ENGLISH DRAMA:
A MODERN VIEWPOINT

FESTIVAL THEATRE CHICHESTER

STRATFORD ONTARIO FESTIVAL (PHOTO HERB NOTT)

ABOVE
The relationship of stage and auditorium in a modern theatre.
The Festival Theatre, Chichester

BELOW *A similar stage at the Festival Theatre, Stratford, Ontario,*
during a performance of HENRY V

ENGLISH DRAMA:

A MODERN VIEWPOINT

by *ALLARDYCE NICOLL*

Decorations by William Bainbridge

GEORGE G. HARRAP & CO. LTD

London Toronto Wellington Sydney

First published in Great Britain 1968
by GEORGE G. HARRAP & CO. LTD
182 High Holborn, London, W.C.1

© *Allardyce Nicoll* 1968
Copyright. All rights reserved

SBN 245 59119 2

Composed in Baskerville (Intertype)
and printed by Willmer Brothers Limited, Birkenhead
Made in Great Britain

Preface

THIS survey has been planned with one specific purpose in view – to provide such an account of English drama as might prove serviceable to those whose principal interest is centred in the modern stage. This means that the survey itself is not to be regarded in any respect as simply a compendious condensation of the subject as a whole. Dramatic developments which seem to have direct or indirect bearing on today's theatrical efforts have been more fully treated, while those having no such bearing have been either completely ignored or else dealt with in a cursory manner. Thus, for example, practically nothing is said about the long line of 'tragic' plays extending from the late seventeenth century well into the nineteenth : not even titles of representative dramas of this sort have been mentioned. For those intent upon tracing theatrical history these works, once the vehicles of a Thomas Betterton, a David Garrick, a Sarah Siddons, a Charles Macready, have definite significance and well deserve to be minutely scrutinized, but for today's playgoers, actors, and directors they can possess not the slightest value. On the other hand an attempt has here been made to stress any aspects in the drama of the past which may seem to have a direct relationship with the present or which may aid in setting modern achievements in perspective.

For this book, therefore, *English Drama: a Modern Viewpoint* appeared to be the only appropriate title : it has been designed as a survey, but a survey in which today has been kept constantly in mind while recording yesterday's dramatic activities.

I wish to thank the following for permission to quote from

copyright works: Messrs Eyre and Spottiswoode, Ltd, for a passage from *The Theatre of the Absurd,* by Martin Esslin; Messrs Methuen and Co., Ltd, for passages from *The Homecoming,* by Harold Pinter; *The Observer,* for passages from articles by Noël Coward, Michael Frayne, and Ronald Bryden; Penguin Books, Ltd, for passages from *The Waters of Babylon,* by John Arden; and *World Theatre,* the magazine of the International Theatre Institute, for passages from an interview with George Devine, which appeared in Vol. XIII, 1964.

My thanks are also due to E. Martin Browne for information concerning recent performances of medieval plays.

A. N.

Contents

1

Ancient and Modern

THE number of plays which the theatre has produced during the long centuries of its history is legion, and most of these are now forgotten. Even if we confine our attention to the English stage alone we are confronted by thousands upon thousands of tragedies, comedies, and farces which either made a brief, undistinguished strut and fret on the boards or, in some instances, after winning temporary applause from the spectators for whom they were written, promptly faded into oblivion. Many of these have vanished utterly, leaving only their titles as records of their one-time existence, but, even so, a vast multitude remain in printed texts. For students of theatrical history the sixteenth- and seventeenth-century quartos and folios, the more manageable eighteenth-century octavos, the flimsy little eye-straining texts issued by Duncombe, Lacy, Dick, and French during the nineteenth century all have lively interest –

so much interest, indeed, that we do not now have to go to one of the larger libraries in order to peruse them: in microfilm and in microprint they are available almost everywhere.

But, we may well ask, for ordinary theatregoers, for actors and for producers, what value can these possibly have? The question is a pertinent one, for two reasons. First, it must be admitted that the majority of these extant plays are of little real worth; there is no reason why we might wish them returned to the stage. And, secondly, it has to be recognized that, in all periods of theatrical activity, audiences in general, together with those professionally concerned with playhouse affairs, have primarily been interested in plays written by their contemporaries; when they turn to the past they direct their attention only to the minute percentage of earlier plays whose authors had been granted the rare power of stepping over the frontiers of their own periods and of speaking in familiar terms to later generations.

Such dramatic works are to be counted by the dozens and not by the thousands, and their numbers are not likely to be materially increased. Very occasionally some enterprising producer may discover a long-forgotten drama, put it on the stage, and win acclaim; but such instances occur only seldom. For practical purposes we may say that we now know all the stageworthy plays created by the English theatre of the past; and their authors form a tiny company of the elect. Shakespeare, clearly, is their leader: the vibrant voice which speaks in *Hamlet* and *Twelfth Night* sounds almost startlingly modern, and there has always been a public eager and anxious to listen to its tones. Yet even here distinctions have to be made. When we utter the word 'Shakespeare' in connection with the playhouse we rarely have in mind the entire contents of the famous First Folio; in effect, we think only of about ten dramas in all; *Titus Andronicus* and the three parts of *King Henry VI* hardly occur to us, and with them there vanish memories of the immature *Two Gentlemen of Verona*, the strangely perplexing *All's Well that Ends Well*, the unsatisfying *King John*. The entire range of Shakespeare's works, of course, has at various times been put upon the stage, and once or twice some almost completely neglected play, such as *Titus Andronicus*, has received temporary acclaim through the skill of director and actor; but this fact does not confute the general truth that even 'Shakespeare', in so far as the contemporary theatre is concerned, means no more than half a score of selected dramas. And when we pass beyond Shakespeare we must remain astonished at realizing how meagre is the proportion of earlier dramatic writings which still hold their own. At one time Ben Jonson's star shone brightly, wellnigh as brilliant as that of Shakespeare, yet for many years now its radiance has gone; when a *Volpone* or an *Every Man in His Humour* is revived its appeal is strictly limited; we may admire the author's ingenuity and esteem his sense of purpose and still fail to be completely captured by his creation. The highly spiced feasts of wit concocted by Etherege and Congreve continue to give delight, and delight, too, can come from listening to Sheridan's scintillating satire and to the mellow humour of Goldsmith; from various periods one or two other plays can similarly be found to retain their interest – indeed, what may have been the very first dramatic text printed in England, the penetrating *Everyman*, may hold us silently arrested by its simple verities and ritualistic movement. When all the harvesting has been done, however, we find in our hands the scripts of only some forty or fifty dramas from the past which might be described as current, familiarly known, and invested with the power of seizing upon and holding our attention on the stage. About the same number may occasionally be given short revivals, usually by amateur societies or on festival occasions, but the basic fact remains that, as audiences and as actors, we are concerned principally with the contemporary; when we leave the company of new plays we stretch out our hands into previous centuries towards only a sadly limited few.

This being so, it might readily seem as though the past could be of no worth or service to us. Unquestionably, we might argue, the history of the theatre and drama has interest, but an interest confined within its own field, and having little or nothing to do with the living playhouse of our own times. In general, we might continue, the truth is that, allowing for the select exceptions, only the modern can appeal to a modern world.

Let us suppose that, with some such thoughts in our minds, we happen to visit a friend who has his bookshelves filled with printed plays old and new. Idly we cast our eyes over the backs of the volumes and on one we note the name of an author unknown to us, John Marston. We take out the book and open it at the reproduction of an old title-page: *The History of Antonio and Mellida*, we read, *The first part. As it hath beene sundry times acted, by the children of Paules, 1602*. Remembering the players scene in *Hamlet*, we realize that this must have been part of the repertory of those little eyases who, having then become the fashion, were berattling the common stages and driving the adult actors to take to the road. We then turn to the text and dip into its dialogue – just that and no more, because the few lines we peruse seem to us positively ludicrous in their artificiality and incompetence. When our friend enters the room maybe we take occasion to tell him what rubbish is here. "This," we say, "is absolutely absurd."

Nevertheless, our use of this very word 'absurd' persuades us to pause for a moment, since we know that the phrase "Theatre of the Absurd" is now being so freely applied, in laudatory terms, to a large area of our own 'modern' drama. And, in having made that pause, when we are alone again we allow our thoughts to go further. Obviously, in considering the revolutionary stages active during the past ten years, we can clearly discern amid all their diversity a number of prevailing trends, to many of which new critical terms have come to be attached. "Theatre of the Absurd" is merely one of these, as is the later phrase "Theatre of Cruelty". When we read articles on the modern playhouse, or when we hear debates on the subject, our eyes and ears become accustomed to words such as 'commitment', 'involvement', 'ambivalence', 'anti-theatre', and 'alienation'; if the argument tends towards the philosophical, then 'anti-Aristotelian' sums up everything. And at this no surprise need be felt, since, although all these phrases and terms have different meanings, they all combine in an attack upon that kind of play-structure which had held the stage from the time when the ancient Greek philosopher, by the exercise of his logic, succeeded in determining and in codifying its main features.

For Aristotle, 'plot', 'character', logical sequence were the true qualities to be sought in a serious drama, leading towards an emotional involvement in the action by those watching its scenes unfold. Opposed to this concept, the advanced 'modern' drama has been inclined to minimize, or even to omit, the plot element in a play, to seek out absurd situations, to shatter the boundaries between tragedy and farce, to work constantly within the sphere of paradox, to devise episodes and language likely to shock the audience, to destroy illusion, to dwell much on the themes of life's fleeting brevity and the perplexing discordances of sexual emotions, often to indulge in a sort of 'private' language – either one belonging to a limited group or else one peculiar to the authors' personal experiences and inner tensions – and to exhibit, at the same time, a strangely vocal moral intensity.

All of this appears entirely new and modern, and we are tempted to believe that it characteristically reflects the spirit of an age unlike any age in the historical past. Here is the dramatic mirror which shows us the basic absurdities of present-day men, able to achieve undreamed-of wonders by the application of their scientific imagination and yet the constant prey of devouring thoughts and passions: here are the human beings so proud of their ability to communicate with each other, delineated in such a manner as to demonstrate the meaninglessness of their common talk; here are the men and women, outwardly logical and 'sensible', who are victims of psychological and social irrationalities; here, in fact, is a vision of man and his universe which may seem entirely new and fresh.

Such considerations pass through our minds as we reflect on our own use of the word 'absurd' with reference to Marston's play and on its current critical use with reference to modern dramatic writings. Obviously these uses are not the same. When we said that Marston's lines were absurd we meant, of course, that we deemed them so foolish as to be unworthy of notice; when we speak of "theatre of the absurd", on the other hand, we imply that the authors concerned are worthily exploiting something which had not been, and could not have been, exploited in the past. Nevertheless, let us suppose that our considerations, despite our recognition of the two senses in which the word 'absurd' has been applied, have the effect of tempting us once more to take that volume of Marston's plays from the shelf on which we had irritatedly thrust it back, and that we sit down to read through his two-part drama.

The first part, *Antonio and Mellida*, might be described as a satirical romantic comedy. The 'story', such as it is, begins to the accompaniment of martial sounds. Andrugio, Duke of Genoa, and his son Antonio – who appears improbably dressed as an Amazon – have, we learn, been defeated by Piero, Duke of Venice. Ridiculous incident follows ridiculous incident. Still in his Amazonian outfit, Antonio insinuates himself into the Venetian Court, reveals his identity to his lover Mellida, and carries her off; she is captured by Piero; at the end, Andrugio, clad in full armour, surrenders himself and displays to Piero a coffin apparently containing the lifeless corpse of his son; suddenly, however, Antonio springs to his feet; whereupon, quite unexpectedly, Piero turns from bitter hatred of his Genoese enemies to an open-hearted welcome.

If this were all we should have had full confirmation for our dismissal of the play as a worthless piece of dramatic folly; yet our more careful reading has brought to attention several puzzling and disturbing elements in its composition. On the surface the plot deals with a rather stupid romantic comedy theme, but we note that its opening is of a very strange sort. The initial stage-direction in itself is peculiar:

Enter Galeatzo, Piero, Alberto, Antonio, Forobosco, Balurdo, Matzagente & Feliche, with parts in their hands, having cloaks cast over their apparel.

Alberto speaks:

<blockquote>
Come, sirs, come: the music will sound straight for entrance. Are ye ready, are ye perfect?

Piero: Faith, we can say our parts; but we are ignorant in what mould we must cast our actors.

Alberto: Whom do you personate?

Piero: Piero, Duke of Venice.

Alberto: O ho: then thus frame your exterior shape
To haughty form of elate majesty,
As if you held the palsy-shaking head
Of reeling chance under your fortune's belt
In strictest vassalage: grow big in thought,
As swoln with glory of successful arms.

Piero: If that be all, fear not: I'll suit it right.
Who can not be proud, stroke up the hair,
and strut?
</blockquote>

Alberto: Truth, such rank custom is grown popular,
And now the vulgar fashion strides as wide,
And stalks as proud, upon the weakest stilts
Of the slight'st fortunes, as if Hercules
Or burly Atlas shoulder'd up their state.

At the very start, then, we are thrust into the midst of what looks like an 'anti-theatre' world, where all is being done to prevent the audience's involvement in the action. The atmosphere thus invoked continues all through this opening scene; at its close the actor taking the part of Antonio turns to the player cast for that of Feliche: "I have heard that those persons, as he and you, Feliche, that are but slightly drawn in this comedy should receive more exact accomplishment in a Second Part." And the same mood is called forth sporadically in the actual scenes of the play itself: at one moment, for example, Antonio and Mellida are suddenly, and inexplicably, made to break off from their English dialogue to speak in Italian — whereupon one of the other characters is permitted to step out of his part, making direct comment to the spectators in critical terms:

If I should sit in judgment, 'tis an error easier to be pardoned by the auditors than excused by the authors; and yet some private respect may rebate the edge of the keener censure.

On hearing a remark such as this we begin to wonder whether all is as it might appear to be on the surface; perhaps, we think, the dramatist was not so naïve as we had imagined, perhaps some 'private respect' may have urged him to pen his seemingly stupid scenes.

As soon as this thought comes to us we recall that within the course of the romantic action we have been suddenly startled by encountering bitter denunciations of the evils and stupidities of the world — denunciations cast in terms of physical nausea and sounding as though they were expressions of the author's own disgust. Such speeches are not put into the mouth of a single character; they are widely spread over the play. Feliche cries out :

O that the stomach of this queasy age
Digests or brooks such raw unseasoned gobs,
And vomits them not forth!

but it is Andrugio who tells us that his

> thoughts are fixed in contemplation
> Why this huge earth, this monstrous animal,
> That eats her children, should not have eyes and ears.

And, as though the author wished to underline the relationship of these two elements in his play, Alberto, in his final speech, is made to combine them into one:

> I'll go and breathe my woes unto the rocks
> And spend my grief upon the deafest seas. . . .
> Farewell, dear friend, expect no more of me;
> Here ends my part in this love's comedy.

With questions of such kind perplexing us, we proceed to look at the second part of the play, *Antonio's Revenge*. From what has gone before, we expect to have a continuation of the queer and disturbing romantic comedy spirit presented in the first part of the play; but here a surprise awaits us, for Marston evidently believed in the shock technique. *Antonio's Revenge* abruptly begins with the entry of Piero,

> *unbraced, his arms bare, smeared in blood, a poniard in one hand bloody, and a torch in the other.*

We have already begun to speculate whether, in the first part, the author had not been deliberately exploiting the absurd, and now we feel ourselves being transported from this Theatre of the Absurd to the Theatre of Cruelty. Feliche, we find, instead of being given his promised "more exact accomplishment" in this second portion of the play, is summarily murdered, his place being taken by a villainous Strotzo; Andrugio, also murdered, returns as a ghost; Piero has his tongue torn out; Antonio, after having killed Piero's innocent son Julio, disguises himself as a Fool, and eventually succeeds in slaying his enemy. The prologue, with its heavy affected language, sets the tone for this farrago of revenge and tension, not so very far removed from the tension and revenge exhibited in Dürrenmatt's *The Visit*:

> The rawish dank of clumsy winter ramps
> The fluent summer's vein, and drizzling sleet
> Chilleth the wan bleak cheek of the numb'd earth,
> Whilst snarling gusts nibble the juiceless leaves

The Conspirators unmasked. Scene from Anthony Quayle's production of HENRY V *at Stratford-upon-Avon,* 1951

Falstaff with the Host of the Garter Inn and Pistol in the Stratford, Ontario, production of THE MERRY WIVES OF WINDSOR

From the naked shuddering branch and peels the skin
From off the soft and delicate aspects.
O, now, methinks, a sullen tragic scene
Would suit the time with pleasing congruence.

The visual actions stress the macabre. Curtains are opened to
reveal Feliche's corpse, "stabbed thick with wounds", hanging
from a beam; Andrugio's ghost passes by "tossing his torch
about his head in triumph". The speeches of the characters
sound in dismal harmony. "Now lions' half-clam'd entrails roar
for food," cries Antonio,

Now croaks the toad, and night-crows screech aloud,
Fluttering 'bout casements of departing souls;
Now gape the graves, and through their yawns let loose
Imprison'd spirits to revisit earth;
And now, swart night, to swell thy hour out,
Behold I spurt warm blood in thy black eyes.

No Jimmy Porter could excel this Antonio in self-pity. When
one character remarks that he is "the miserablest soul that
breathes", the hero "starts up" and angrily refutes him:

'Slid, sir, ye lie: by the heart of grief thou liest.
I scorn't that any wretched should survive
Outmounting me in that superlative,
Most miserable, most unmatch'd in woe.

Attired in his disguise as a Fool, "with a little toy of a walnut
shell and soap to make bubbles", he discourses in tones similar
to many we have recently heard on our stage: "Note a Fool's
beatitude," he cries,

He is not capable of passion;
Wanting the power of distinction,
He bears an unturn'd sail with every wind;
Blow east, blow west, he stirs his course alike.
I never saw a Fool lean – the chub-fac'd fop
Shines sleek with full-cramm'd fat of happiness,
Whilst studious contemplation sucks the juice
From wizards' cheeks, who, making curious search
For Nature's secrets, the first innating cause
Laughs them to scorn, as man doth busy apes
When they will zany men. Had heaven been kind,
Creating me an honest senseless dolt,

B

A good poor fool, I should want sense to feel
The stings of anguish shoot through every vein . . .
    I could not thus run mad
As one confounded in a maze of mischief,
Stagger'd, stark fell'd with bruising stroke of chance.

And, while he plays with his walnut shell and soap, his words –
"Puff, hold world; puff, hold bubble; puff, hold world" –
recall the mood of those modern dramatists who want the earth
to stop turning because they would like to get off.

Yet, in spite of all this gloom, the spirit of anti-theatre continues to confront us. Balurdo, for example, after a lengthy
dismal scene of mourning, is made to enter "with a beard half
off, half on"; when Piero comments on this, he replies:

Then I must be forced to conclude the tyring-man hath not
glued on my beard half fast enough.

There would, indeed, seem to be no doubt that we were mistaken in thinking that Marston wrote nonsense because he did
not know any better; while we may still consider him to be a
mediocre playwright, it appears certain that he was well aware
of the absurdities he was engaged in exploiting and that all
his scenes were designed to illustrate his disgusted anger at the
world's follies and uglinesses.

We started out on this inquiry by supposing that, almost at
random, we had pulled an old play from a friend's bookshelves. Now that we have reached a conclusion concerning its
nature and purpose, let us continue with a further supposition
– that, having closed the volume, we sit down for a few minutes
to allow certain questions to pass through our minds.

Marston, we say to ourselves, seems to have been anticipating
what is now known as the Theatre of the Absurd; but what
significance has this for us? The answer to that query must
obviously be "In itself, none at all". There is but little likelihood
that *Antonio and Mellida* will be revived on the stage: the very
fact that such quality as it possesses could be appreciated only
by seeing its two parts acted together might well warrant our
turning 'little likelihood' into 'absolute impossibility'. And
even if it had had stage interest, we realize that the mere dis-

covery of similarities between its style and that of some contemporary dramas could have no real practical value.

The reaching of this conclusion, however, does have the effect of raising a further question: was this old, forgotten two-part play a mere freak, the aberrant product of an eccentric mind? An answer to that query is easily come by: we do not need to turn to any histories of the stage for information; various recent revivals of early seventeenth-century comedies and tragedies, together with the programme notes provided for these productions, and a knowledge of the text of *Hamlet* give us what we need. The revivals show that, although deliberate exhibitions of the absurd may not be common, numerous plays of this period manifest styles akin to that mood, with scenes bitter, angry, and cruel. *Antonio and Mellida*, then, does not stand alone in anticipating our contemporary spirit, and, if we look a little more closely, we must be surprised to find that these plays took form out of conditions which display unexpected resemblances to present-day conditions. Malcontents stride about morosely on stage and off, and the programme notes rightly point out that the malcontent was the counterpart of what now is known as the angry young man. From the same sources we learn that many of the plays, like *Antonio and Mellida*, were written, not for the great public playhouses, but for the more exclusive small 'private' theatres which suddenly sprang into being around the year 1600. And that, of course, immediately brings to mind the well-known passage in *Hamlet*. Announcement is made of the arrival of the players, none other than "the tragedians of the city": the Prince is puzzled as to why they have thus gone on tour as strollers, and Rosencrantz tells him of the "aery of children, little eyases", who

> cry out on the top of question, and are most tyrannically clapped for 't : these are now the fashion, and so berattle the common stages (so they call them) that many wearing rapiers are afraid of goose-quills, and dare scarce come thither.

"Faith," he adds, "there has been much to-do on both sides: and the nation holds it no sin to tarre them to controversy. There was, for a while, no money bid for argument, unless the Poet and the Player went to cuffs in the question." A glance at the appropriate commentary in any annotated edition of

Shakespeare's tragedy indicates that these words formed an unexaggerated comment on the playhouse world at the start of the seventeenth century: there was at that time an open War of the Theatres reminiscent of latter-day declarations of 'frontal war' and of verbal attacks sufficiently choleric to provide newspaper headlines.

Here, then, is something which goes far beyond the limits of a single obscure play. Here is a New Wave which has many points of contact with our own: here are at least some dramas deemed worthy of revival: the scope is wider and the issues are so pertinent as to call for further inquiry. Surely we want to know more about several aspects of this movement – specifically, when did it start? what were the moving forces which brought it into being? amid what conditions did it flourish? and, above all, how long did it endure?

The passage in *Hamlet* raises other considerations. Apart from the fact that it emphasizes the existence of controversy, indicating that not all plays written and produced during those years belonged to one single new style, it brings into the picture a tragedy which is universally regarded as among the greatest of all theatrical achievements, which, indeed, is so powerful as to make it seem no less vital than anything created yesterday or today. There is really no question of a 'revival' of *Hamlet*: *Hamlet* belongs to our living stage.

This thought serves to stress an essential fact – that the theatre, as an art, differs materially from the arts of literature and painting. In these spheres the past obviously has a significance, even a deep significance, both for artists and for public, yet there is a basic difference. Chaucer composes his *Canterbury Tales*, Fielding writes *Tom Jones*, and, if we wish to peruse these works it does not matter whether we read them in sumptuously prepared private-press editions or in cheap reprints: both in the one and in the other the contact between the author and the reader remains identically direct and similar. Giotto paints his frescoes on the walls of the Paduan Scrovegni Chapel; if we wish to study their excellences, there – save for such damage as time may have wrought – they remain for us to see: Leonardo completes his portrait of Mona Lisa, and on a wall in the Louvre it can be contemplated at leisure.

Dramas are different. Naturally we can read *Hamlet* just as we can look at the portrait or at the frescoes, but, whereas they were end-results in themselves, the tragedy was written for performance, and for us the full impact of Shakespeare's vision can be appreciated only in the theatre. Theatrical production, however, means interpretation; and it is precisely here that there arises the greatest question of all. What kind of interpretation do we ideally seek?

Do we, for example, want a presentation of *Hamlet* under conditions as nearly akin as possible to those operative in his own time? The answer must be both a 'Yes' and a 'No'. The affirmative is necessary because of our discovery, during comparatively recent years, that there exists a peculiarly intimate association between the form of Shakespeare's play and the stage for which it was conceived: with mingled amusement and dismay we now look back on Charles Kean's archaeologically spectacular presentations – on the twenty-minute waits while his 140 scene-shifters sweated behind the curtain, on such elaborate expansions of stage-directions as are exemplified by his treatment of "Enter Leontes, Lords and Officers" in *The Winter's Tale*, when audiences were greeted with the mummery of officers of the Court, heralds, ladies, soldiers, sages, squires, priests, trumpeters, 135 in all. We now know that Shakespeare's vision vanishes amid such pageantry. Indeed, we can go further than that and say that one of the most potent forces in the present-day playhouse has been the discovery, in general, of the virtues of the Elizabethan theatre, not only for Shakespeare's works but for our own plays as well.

Our affirmative reply, however, has to be accompanied by a no less emphatic negative. When *Hamlet* is being presented the very last thing we should desire is a dull historical reconstruction of the way in which we think it might have appeared at its *première*. We might have a replica of the Globe; on its stage we might have actors sincerely striving to perform in a supposedly Elizabethan manner; but in the end the impress would be false and forced, failing in its effect if only because the spectators, in all things from accoutrement to conscience, would have obstinately to remain creatures of our own time. Clearly, then, our interpretation must be modern.

The question here is, how modern? It can be argued, quite logically, that a theatrical production stands in its own right, that it is not to be looked upon merely as an interpretation of a play but rather as an art-object possessed of intrinsic individual qualities. If this is so, then it is entirely right and proper for a director, taking into account the prevailing trends of his own time, to treat the selected drama in contemporary terms. Thus, for instance, he can stress such of its aspects as seem to have a modern flavour or he can apply to its entire text a 'modern' conception. Such performances have been common within recent years, and there is hardly need to say that several of them have proved exciting theatrical experiences. At the same time, even while recognizing the logic of the approach and while welcoming the successes, a statement made, only a few months ago, by a prominent Rumanian theatre director must make us pause: "On our stages," he says, "we show Shakespeare and we show Brecht, but we know better than to mix them: we realize that if we were to impose Brecht on Shakespeare, we should lose what Shakespeare has to offer us."

The basis of that remark is, of course, the belief that Shakespeare, one of the mightiest of all authors, has enshrined in each of his more important plays a peculiar vision and that this vision, although conceived almost four centuries ago, has validity and cogency for our time. If this is true what do we want when *Hamlet* is put upon the stage? Clearly something of a compromise, wherein the prime objective would be to make the production such as to appeal in modern terms and yet wherein an effort would be made to stress the Shakespearian vision, and not Brecht's or anybody else's. To achieve that end, some knowledge of the past would be essential, with sufficient awareness of theatrical progress as a whole to guard against over-hasty acceptance of perhaps over-hasty critical statements or historical hypotheses. It is, indeed, very easy to be misled. Let us take as an example the two plays we have been considering. Quite possibly *Hamlet* and *Antonio and Mellida* both made their first appearances during the course of a single season, that of 1600-01 : at any rate, they can have been separated from each other only by a couple of years at most. Probably, in our reading of the latter our attention has been caught by some passages which disturbingly called to mind scenes in Shakespeare's play. We have already come to the conclusion that Marston was deliberately exploiting absurdities. If, therefore, we come across a critical essay which seeks to expound *Hamlet* as being also a drama of the absurd, may we not readily be tempted to seize on the suggestion and make it the core of a production? Only some knowledge of the conditions under which these two works came into being can help us towards reaching a valid conclusion – the one a piece written by a young, reasonably well-to-do university man for the little eyases occupying a private theatre, and the other a tragedy composed by a firmly established and manifestly great actor-author for the most prominent company of the age, performing in the famous Globe playhouse.

For diverse reasons, then, knowledge of the theatre's past would seem to be enriching, perhaps often essential, for all who participate in its current affairs, and these include spectators as well as actors, directors, and scene-designers. In the playhouse, however, time moves swiftly, and often there are few moments of leisure for turning from immediate practice to the perusal of books. Apart from that consideration, there is another associated with it: while the whole of theatrical and dramatic history is interesting, it must be confessed that there are stretches within its scope which have no pertinency for ourselves. In most of the volumes which seek, either briefly or at length, to provide an account of the varying fortunes of the stage throughout the centuries, the tendency has, quite rightly, been to give as much space and weight to what has only historical significance as to what appears to have a direct connection with present-day dramatic activities – and studies of such a kind, even if time is found for their reading, may possibly be found confusing.

With these questions and reflections in mind, therefore, this survey has deliberately been kept as short as possible, and, as has already been emphasized in its preface, it has been prepared with one central objective. Based on the assumption that our chief interest rests in the activities of the contemporary theatre, it concentrates upon those dramatic developments which may have an interest for the present, disregarding entirely or only briefly mentioning other developments which belong entirely to the past. Fundamentally it aims at stimulating several basic questions: what plays from earlier epochs can have real value for us today? What were the conditions which brought them into existence? Can we profit from examining dramatic movements which seem to have some sort of affinity with what is happening in the theatre of today? From conclusions arising out of such comparisons can we aid ourselves towards enhancing our appreciation of current stage offerings? Naturally, the answers given to any such questions are bound to vary, depending upon individual attitudes and concepts: but the very posing of the questions may be thought to be not without its own inherent worth.

2

Plays
of Simple
Faith

We must, naturally, start at the beginning, even although it might seem, at first glance, that this beginning is so far removed, both in time and in spirit, from the world which we now inhabit that it could have but little interest for us. The vast, sprawling range of the medieval religious drama might, indeed, be considered to be something utterly distinct from what we now know, something without any relevance for ourselves. Nevertheless, before we set it aside, we must observe that one of our most prominent theatrical companies has been making plans for a revival of these plays; looking round us, we must see signs that several contemporary dramatists, including even authors associated with the present New Wave, have been casting nostalgic glances backward towards the Middle Ages; and, in addition, we must recognize that unless we have some knowledge of theatrical activity during that period we shall but ill appreciate some of the salient qualities in the plays, including Shakespeare's, which later took its place.

The distancing from the drama of today depends partly on the facts that these medieval plays were designed as vehicles for large numbers of unquestionably sincere, although certainly sometimes incompetent, amateurs and that they were presented only on annual 'festival' occasions. There was, therefore, nothing at that time which corresponds to the present-day theatre, whether commercial or subsidized. The chief cause of the gulf separating the two, however, rests in the wider fact that those plays were the creations of an age utterly unlike our own. Physically and spiritually the England of that period differed in wellnigh every respect from the largely urban, industrialized England of 1968. It was then a land of scattered communities, diminutive villages, and tiny towns, where time moved slowly and travel could, in general, be effected only by toilsome passage on foot over stony tracks: even London, the largest centre and housing the royal Court, was no more than a sparsely populated borough.

Politically, the people were distracted and at times decimated by intestine battles between rival factions of the feudal lords, but in the realm of religious belief all were united. Although men might at times jest coarsely over their cups about things sacred and ecclesiastical, there were in effect no atheists, no dissenters: all accepted the same beliefs, and, while there might be some debate concerning the relative powers of Church and State, everyone bowed to the one Catholic authority with its seat in Rome. Recognizing man's weakness, this supreme spiritual institution, to our eyes foolishly yet perhaps not without wisdom from its own point of view, restrained individual 'scientific' investigation as much as it could, and in its control lay primarily the interpretation of truth. The religious concept, thus expounded, was a truly living thing: God was real, and the power of devils omnipresent: the events narrated in the Bible seemed to men as though they had happened yesterday, so that the numerous crusades from 1096 on to the closing years of the thirteenth century, when princes and nobles and men-at-arms were willing to suffer the miseries of long, difficult voyages and the torments of desert heat, did not seem to be inspired so much by a desire to capture ancient monuments from the Saracens as to preserve an immediate continuity with a vital Jerusalem.

It was within this milieu that, about a century before the earliest crusade, the first diminutive dramatic seedling suddenly sprouted within the confines of the Church. Here, however, we must be perfectly frank: with our present purpose in view, the entire story of that seedling's slow growth during the following three or four centuries may here be wholly neglected. The primitive Latin liturgical plays, simple expansions of Easter and Christmas services, offer us nothing of practical significance, and in England at least we encounter virtually no development likely to make us pause until we reach the great cycles of mystery dramas which took shape about the time when Richard II was holding colourful Court and bringing himself to disaster.

These plays we cannot ignore. 'Cycles' they are usually called because they consist of collections of short episodes designed to display the significant events narrated in the Old and New Testaments – the Creation of the World, the Expulsion of Adam and Eve from Paradise, the Sin of Cain, the Building of the Ark, Christ's Birth, Crucifixion, and Resurrection. Some of the playlets inclined towards only vaguely dramatic action, with long stretches of largely narrative verse; some put forward their stories in attenuated, but often appealingly human, terms; some were sanctioned to include elements of comedy among their serious actions, as when Noah's wife, a familiar shrew, treats her husband as a stupid old fool, when the torturers indulge in grim humour while they strain the cords on the Cross, or when the soldiers utter their jests in dice-tossing for Christ's garments; and a very few pieces, such as the second shepherd's piece in the so-called Wakefield cycle, exhibit attempts to achieve more complex structure. This last example is sufficiently important to warrant more than a passing glance. The greater part of the play is pure invention, with no reference whatsoever to the Biblical story: before us we see a group of shepherds huddling round an open fire as they guard their flocks and we listen to them enviously comparing their own miserable lot with the comforts enjoyed by those of gentler birth; out of the darkness slinks in a thievish rascal named Mak who pathetically begs to warm himself in their company, and who, when they fall asleep, repays their rather grudging hospitality by stealing a lamb; wakening and discovering their loss, they track down the miscreant to his tumbledown cottage, discover the lamb wrapped up in a cradle, and for his sins toss the thief in a blanket. Then, with startling suddenness in the midst of their jeering laughter, a great star shines down from the heavens while an angelic chorus hymns the birth of the Lamb of God, to whose humble stable they troop with their rustic gifts. Even for those who have now lost their faith, the dramatic moulding of this short play has a strange appealing intensity.

In considering these mystery cycles, two things have to be kept firmly in our minds. The first is that the individual play-lets, whether primitively semi-narrative or, as in this shepherds' piece, displaying a real sense of 'theatre', were not in them-selves separate entities, that they were definitely planned as parts of a larger whole; and the second is that they were crea-tions of a community spirit, sponsored by the trade-guilds, per-formed in such a way as to render 'actors' and 'spectators' almost indistinguishable. For those who essayed the speaking rôles and for the villagers or townsfolk who formed the watch-ing public, these mystery cycles represented undeniable truth, truth which had profound and intimate pertinence for every man, woman, and child. Master John Jones, blacksmith by trade, who ranted and roared as King Herod, and Master Peter Smith the tailor, who suffered as Christ, were fellows and pos-sibly boon tavern companions of the crowd watching their per-formances, but for the moment these ordinary men became the real King of Israel and the true Jesus. Still further, when Christ was led to Calvary, not only was this journey a matter of deep concern for the participants, the spectators became mys-teriously transformed into the very crowd who had been pre-sent at the historical scene centuries before. In effect, the then and the now were merged into one, exactly as we see them com-bined in medieval frescoes and miniatures. Sometimes we hear this drama of the Middle Ages described as 'didactic', but the use of that term tends to obscure its inner quality: no doubt at the start it was largely designed to give an unlettered public living images of cardinal episodes in the Bible, but a deeper appreciation of the effect created by the performances of the mystery cycles is more likely to be gained by regarding them as a sort of re-enactment of events fundamental for Everyman.

While intimate and detailed investigation of medieval drama is a fascinating field of study, even when we reach these larger and more fully expanded mystery plays nothing more is needed, from the purely practical point of view, than the few basic facts outlined above. Nevertheless, certain conclusions and knowledge of some other facts concerning the staging of the plays have immediate interest for us.

An understanding of the methods of production is, indeed, fundamental, and the scope of these methods can be comprehended only by thinking first of the nature of the dramatic material included in the cycles. Clearly, each of the individual parts had its own appropriate locality: from His house in heaven God created the world, Adam and Eve dwelt in a terrestrial paradise, Christ was born in Bethlehem, damned souls were tortured in hell. Still further, even the contracted scope of individual plays had to allow for fictional travelling from place to place, with the consequent invoking of several distinct localities within the course of the action: in the Wakefield shepherds' play, for example, there is the scene on the moor, then Mak's cottage, and finally the stable where the child Christ lies. In order to deal with such an extended area of physical action and of fictional places the medieval performers developed a system consisting of two basic elements – they used small platforms, generally called 'mansions' or 'pageants', with symbolic decorations to indicate their supposed qualities, and, in addition, they kept a free open space, named the 'platea' or 'place', between themselves and their audiences. Thus one little stage with a formalized representation of a temple might stand for Jerusalem, and if the nature of the play demanded another locality the actors could step down onto the 'place' and, through their dialogue, signify that they had moved out of the city and come to another spot; in an inversion of this procedure the shepherds might start in the 'place' with their encampment, pretend later that Mak's cottage was at the side of the 'pageant' and, at the end, step up on the platform which was supposed to be the stable with its manger. Sometimes the 'pageants' were put upon wheels, so that they might be pulled from position to position as required; sometimes they were all set up together in semicircles, circles, or other formations; but, no matter how they

were arranged, the general principles remained – platforms
provided for the more important localities and a 'place' which
might fancifully serve for almost anything. In essence, then, the
medieval staging was formal, conventional, non-realistic. For
this audience the image of Paradise was so real and vivid that
no theatrical 'reality' was required for its representation.

It hardly needs to be said that in this method of presentation
is to be found the inspiration for the Shakespearian stage, and,
when we think of the influence of that stage upon contemporary
dramatic activities, we realize that here is something which,
although removed by many centuries in time, is in fact very
close to us. The principles upon which it was based are, in fact,
those which have been seen in many modern productions.

Before leaving the question of the medieval staging methods
one other suggestion may be made. As is well known, the development of religious representations during the Middle Ages
was thoroughly international, but there is one distinction which
maybe ought to be drawn between the production of mystery
plays in England and the production of similar plays in France
and in Italy. We must say 'maybe', since records of the former
are fragmentary and often inconclusive, whereas for continental performances fairly rich documentation is extant: yet, after
making all allowances, we are forced to assume that French
and Italian audiences sought for, and were given, more elaborate decorative effects than were offered to the English public.
In those other countries the display seems often to have been
much more spectacular; greater time and effort appears to have
been devoted to pictorial embellishments and far subtler ingenuity applied to what the French called *feyntes*. If this conclusion is correct, then we may well believe that the English
spectators were induced to give closer attention to the poetic
dialogue than to what was presented to their eyes. This might
be put in another way by suggesting that throughout those
long centuries audiences were being trained to listen, and to
exercise their imaginations, and that this training helped to
provide a foundation for the later accomplishments of the
Elizabethan theatre.

This thought brings us back from the staging to the plays
themselves, and when we look at these in connection with
present-day theatrical activities it becomes evident that, al-

though at first we might have believed any direct association between the one and the other would have been impossible, memories of the medieval are still active and influential among us. Festival productions of plays selected from the various extant larger cycles have charmed and moved summer audiences, and other productions of these plays in churches have been encouraged by the work of the Religious Drama Society under the active presidency of E. Martin Browne. And still more important than such revivals have been the productions of plays newly written for performance under ecclesiastical auspices. T. S. Eliot's *Murder in the Cathedral* (1935) was originally composed for presentation at Canterbury; Christopher Fry's *A Sleep of Prisoners* (1950) was similarly conceived for performance in church; and it is indeed significant that one of the leaders of the New Wave of dramatists, John Arden, has followed the same line in his *Business of Good Government* (1963).

Although these and other recent writings rightly veer away from the medieval pattern both in content and approach, they all stem directly from contemplation of the drama of the Middle Ages; and alongside of them stand others, not 'religious' in subject-matter, which indirectly have been inspired by the same process of contemplation. After writing his *Business of Good Government*, John Arden, in collaboration with Margaretta Darcy, has produced a children's play in a new style, *The Royal Pardon* (1966), and during the same season appeared a piece of a similar kind, *The Thwarting of Baron Bolligrew*, from the pen of another young dramatist, Robert Bolt. Why did these writers, quite independently, turn to this kind of composition? In all probability one critic was right in suggesting that the first was inspired "with the aim of finding some modern equivalent for the community drama of the Middle Ages", and it seems likely that in writing the second play Bolt rejoiced in the opportunity of creating plot, theme, characters, and dialogue for appreciation at various levels. If that is indeed so, then the ancient cycles and their conditions of staging may have a value for us quite apart from their own texts and from attempts to revive them.

In any event, whether or not these latest writings by Arden and Bolt were thus inspired, it is important – indeed, obligatory – to give due attention to this medieval drama, both because it was the fount from which the Elizabethan drama flowed and because its approach, although at first appearing to be unexcitingly primitive, was in fact based on firm principles which have had a seminal force in the theatre of today.

3

Interludes, Merry and Moral

VERY often, even if we have sought to learn something about the medieval drama, we are inclined to skip almost everything from the middle of the fifteenth century on to the year 1588, when Christopher Marlowe cleaved the general air with the high-astounding terms of his *Tamburlaine*. If we do look at one or two plays between these dates, as likely as not our attention will be directed to the tragic action of *Gorboduc*, written by Thomas Sackville and Thomas Norton in 1562, to the comic rusticities of *Gammer Gurton's Needle*, penned by a certain 'Mr S.' shortly before, and to the intrigues of Nicholas Udall's *Ralph Roister Doister*, of about the same vintage.

An abrupt sweeping forward from the mystery cycles to Marlowe, however, is decidedly inadvisable, since the intermediate period was fundamentally formative: it may have no buried riches, but an understanding of what was happening

C

during that epoch is essential. And any concentration on the efforts of Sackville, Norton, 'Mr S.', and Udall must inevitably result in distortion, and that for several reasons. Their three plays were amateur ventures: *Gorboduc* was prepared by a couple of well-born authors for performance by their fellow-gentlemen at the Inner Temple; *Gammer Gurton's Needle* was a Cambridge play; *Ralph Roister Doister* was designed by a schoolmaster for presentation by his pupils. It is important to observe that, while all three are unquestionably interesting and indeed important dramatic achievements for their time, they lie outside the main development of the sixteenth-century theatre. What matters for us is the central deepening professional tradition from which eventually Shakespeare arose; and in order to appreciate the force of that tradition we have to direct our gaze away from these and kindred efforts, turning still further backward in time and extending our range.

Shakespeare, as everyone is aware, was a professional actor and part-owner of the great Globe playhouse; his writings were planned for interpretation, not by gentlemen amateurs, school-boys or students, but by men who were proud of their attachment to the 'quality' of player; men of substance they were, and their company, originally vaunting the title of the Lord Chamberlain's Servants, later was elevated in status as the King's Men. The conditions surrounding them and their position in the social world were utterly unlike anything to be found in the Middle Ages; nevertheless, these conditions and that position were not entirely a sudden innovation during the last years of Queen Elizabeth's reign. Behind these actors stretched a long hundred-years-old line of professionalism which, starting from humble beginnings, gradually built up the corporate spirit and expertize from which the later companies drew their assurance and their skill.

The detailed history of this movement need not concern us, but a general idea of what happened is essential if we are to appreciate what developed later. About the middle of the fifteenth century come the earliest records of royal 'players of interludes', and very soon other records demonstrate that divers nobles were hastening to follow their monarchs' lead by engaging troupes of their own. Throughout the better part of a century, however, these companies remained truly diminutive, consisting usually of only three men and a boy – the boy being necessary for the taking of feminine rôles. At first, no doubt, the players, as 'servants' of their lords, restricted their activities to the palaces and castles to which they were attached, but at an early date they began to extend their field of operation. Their masters probably found that, while it was convenient to have these actors on call at Christmastide and similar festive occasions, they could save money by allowing the companies to earn their keep by performing elsewhere as well. Thus gradually the attachment to particular lords tended to become titular rather than real, and thus, too, the actors, turned into strollers, were given an opportunity of enlarging their experience. In the later drama of *Sir Thomas More* (about 1595) there is a pleasant little historical picture which illustrates their procedure. More is giving a banquet for some distinguished guests; the Lord Cardinal's players opportunely come to offer their service, which is eagerly accepted; from their repertory the host chooses an interlude of *The Marriage of Wit and Wisdom* for the occasion. Not only gentlemen, however, could find delight in these performances, and soon we get glimpses of the actors in humbler surroundings, playing sometimes in the open among village communities, sometimes indoors when an inn or a civic hall could be made available for their use.

The story of the professionals' early wanderings has, of course, only factual interest; but interest of a different kind comes before us as we turn to consider the kind of drama and of histrionic interpretation resultant from the conditions within which they carried on their activities. Obviously, these small companies stood apart, in every respect, from the medieval amateurs: the latter had had little opportunity of developing an artistic tradition, since they took their parts only at limited annual holiday periods, whereas the former were only too anxious to keep busily employed all the year round; the amateurs had no thought of profit-making or material personal gain, and consequently, although no doubt they did seriously try to do their best, they did not have to keep their eyes constantly on their audiences, whereas the professionals knew that they could not expect to attract much money unless they truly pleased the public; the amateurs were aware that, when Corpus Christi day came along, the trade-guilds would bring out their pageants, their costumes, and their properties, whereas the strollers, for their part, were equally well aware that in their trudgings along rutted lanes the most they could carry with them in their packs were a few theatrical suits and a bare minimum of essential hand-props. For them, therefore, the old mystery cycles were in every respect unsuited; not only did those Biblical plays demand for their representation scores of eager amateurs working under the aegis and with the active assistance of the guilds, they were designed as day-long performances amid festival conditions. What the new professionals required was something entirely different – a repertory of short, independent plays of such a kind as were likely to appeal to, and hence to bring in money from, both noble patrons and general public, plays, moreover, which, apart from being short and entertaining, could be performed anywhere, inside or outside, with practically no theatrical gear.

The answer to the actors' problem was found in the cultivation of those characteristic playlets which usually were called 'interludes' – a term which seems to have been almost exclusively restricted to England and which, despite its occasional application to similar short pieces performed by schoolboys and by enthusiastic gentlemen amateurs, appears prevailingly to have had the specific significance of a dramatic text cast in the shape demanded by the professional players. Looking round them, watching their audiences, these actors could easily have sensed the tastes and interests of the age: the public was much occupied with serious doctrinal, political, and moral problems and yet it rejoiced in such rough kinds of merriment as are reflected in the popular jest-books of the period: Sir Thomas More was certainly an extraordinary man, and yet he might well be regarded as ordinarily symbolic, ever ready for a laugh, intent on moral issues, willing ultimately to go to the scaffold for his faith. The age, too, was one which had inherited from its medieval predecessors a liking for allegory, for presentation and discussion of larger issues in terms of personifications, for the sight of conflicts between the Vices and the Virtues. And thus, in seeking to give the public what it wanted, the actors generally made up their repertory of interludes introducing serious plots in which Mankind or Youth was swayed towards evil by Lust and Gluttony and drawn towards virtue by Contrition and Repentance, while at the same time providing spectators with laughable and uproarious scenes often centring upon a stock figure called the Vice, sometimes malevolent but more frequently just a-moral, amusing, and roguish – the ancestor of Falstaff and Autolycus. True, some interludes were entirely solemn, although it is to be suspected that most of these, like *Everyman* (about 1500), had associations with amateurs rather than with professionals; true, also, some of these playlets depended wholly upon merriment; but the majority were of a mixed sort, presenting "a tedious brief scene" and "very tragical mirth".

If we think of these interludes as one-act plays, each running from half an hour to about an hour, we might readily believe that any given specimen of the type would be limited to a single fictional locality and that it would include no more characters than the number of actors available for its performance. In point of fact, neither players nor public made any such demands: a single short interlude might have three or four quite separate places of action, and, even although it was familiarly known that the companies consisted of only four actors, the text might call for the appearance of some nine or ten individual characters. Nor was this procedure due to mere incompetence or thoughtlessness. The fact that numerous title-pages indicate how the nine or ten dramatis personae might be doubled in such a way as to make the piece 'easily' playable by four actors shows that the extension in space and scope was quite deliberate. This English public during the first part of the sixteenth century sought for no limiting classical restrictions.

The players' procedure was simplicity itself. In presenting their interludes in baronial hall or on village green they asked for nothing except a small acting-area and the assistance of the audience's imagination. If there were hall doors behind them, these no doubt were used; if there was a musicians' gallery above, that also might be brought into service; but essentially they had taught themselves how, when the occasion arose, to do without any special equipment. And, in thus teaching themselves, they likewise taught their audiences. The plays, for instance, calling for doubling, and in a short piece in which three men and a boy had to interpret half a score of characters clearly there could not be much time for costume changes:

in practice what happened was that the spectators came to accept the slightest quick alteration in apparel (let us say, a cloak hurriedly cast over the shoulders) or of facial appearance (often just a false beard clipped on) as establishing personalities different from those represented immediately before by the same actors. Nor was this acceptance simply something forced upon the public by the conditions of performance: not only did the spectators agree to the conventional doubling made necessary by the smallness of the companies, they went out of their way to encourage the actors to indulge in numerous deliberate disguisings within the course of the action.

This attitude of the audiences towards the conventions employed by the players is, of course, embraced within the relationship persisting between the players and their public and within the whole attitude of the latter to the pieces being presented before them. In the performances of the medieval mystery cycles, as we have seen, those who took the speaking rôles were simply members of the community who happened to have been chosen to represent the Biblical characters, while the crowd standing round the pageants became part of what was not so much a play as a re-enactment of ancient events. Now, however, with the development of the professional interluders, the actors were distinct and set apart from those before whom they performed; and the public, not involved in episodes intimately and deeply familiar, but watching plays whose content had been invented, necessarily were turned into spectators interested in novel stories.

This, however, does not in any sense imply that they were in a position akin to that occupied by audiences in nineteenth-century picture-frame theatres. Here they stood in the hall of a mansion, on the same level as the actors and in the same light, only a few feet separating the entertainers and the entertained. Nor were there any scenic embellishments within the area occupied by the performers to make a distinction between 'stage' and 'auditorium'. The conventions employed in the presentation of the action were so simple and easy that the audience's imagination was left free both to look upon the scenes as though they were things strange and to share in their episodes. In examining the texts of these plays we get the impression that the more serious parts inclined on the whole to the former attitude whereas ample scope was allowed for the comic characters, and especially for the Vice, to keep in close and intimate contact with the public. In reading these lighter scenes we sense that the performers must have freely indulged in just such a technique as is brilliantly exhibited today in Frankie Howerd's approach to his audiences. The interluders are constantly addressing the spectators directly, asking their advice, referring to them for confirmation of their assertions, singling out individuals in the 'Naughty! You're mocking!' style, even pushing their way through the crowd, sometimes with a moderately polite request for 'Room!', sometimes in a manner more rudely boisterous.

A dividing line comes about the middle of the century, but it was not a line which marked a reaction to or a revolt against the traditions operative during the earlier years: rather should it be regarded as an expansive development growing out of the methods employed by the first small professional companies. As the years passed by these men succeeded in gathering a playgoing public sufficiently large to provide them with adequate takings; thus they found it possible to increase their personnel, and such enlargement in their numbers meant that they were granted the opportunity of producing dramas considerably lengthier than the short interludes with which alone their predecessors had been able to cope.

And at last came the time when, in 1576, the actors were possessed of such an extended repertory and had gained such a wide appreciative hearing from London's citizens as to permit them to consider a transformation of their hitherto chiefly nomadic life into a settled one – and, in particular, to dream of building and occupying a home of their own. The first permanent public playhouse, called simply "The Theatre", was, it is true, a venture privately financed by James and Cuthbert Burbage, but we must believe that, with an undertaking so novel and of such significance, the performers joined with the sponsors in devoting serious and careful thought to its architectural form. These men were of considerable practical experience; they were well acquainted with what the spectators wanted and it was in their interest to improve the conditions of their work; some of them assuredly knew of the way in which the Italian scenic theatre was spreading its influence among various European countries, and indeed all of them were bound to be familiar with the related pictorial settings which, as will be seen, were being cultivated by gentlemen amateurs and by child-actors under the direct encouragement of their Queen. We may, therefore, confidently assume that The Theatre of 1576 did not have its structural features determined by chance: what its builders did and what they did not do are of almost equal significance.

We might readily have supposed that the actors would have hired or caused to be erected a rectangular playhouse of proportions similar to those of the baronial halls to which they and their predecessors had become accustomed; and we might also have supposed that they would have been eager to be as up-to-date as possible by making provision for some kind of scenic display. Instead, applying their first-hand knowledge of the various conditions under which they had so successfully acted, they invented an entirely new theatrical form, which, however, incorporated the essential elements in their accustomed theatrical environment. If only because this Elizabethan playhouse has played, and is still playing, such a potent rôle in our own times, a summary of its chief principles is essential.

First, for commercial reasons, the actors wished the building to accommodate as large a number of spectators as possible, and yet, for other reasons, they wanted to keep these spectators as close as they could to the acting-area. The circular or polygonal plan exemplified in The Theatre and in its immediate successors – The Swan, The Rose, and The Globe – with their enclosing galleries and with their platform stages jutting out into the yards, was clearly the best answer to their basic problem. Secondly, the players naturally knew that they must provide for themselves appropriate means of getting upon the stage, and since they had been in the habit, when acting indoors, of making their entrances and exits through the passage-ways leading into the halls, they set up at the rear of the platform a façade somewhat akin to the 'screen' which was a permanent feature in so many mansions. The doors in this screen, or façade, no doubt served them for most of their goings to and fro, but there is reason to believe that, remembering the manner in which the Vice and other characters had pushed their way at times through the groups of assembled onlookers, they were also prepared to make provision for other entries when an actor might come in at the side of the platform, on the yard level, and 'pass over the stage'. Thirdly, the performers had probably discovered by this time that on occasion it was very convenient to act in front of a screen wherein the openings were provided with curtains or hangings, and therefore their theatre façade was constructed in such a way as to permit the introduction of a relatively small inner acting-area. Precisely how this inner stage was contrived – whether revealed by the opening of a large central door or whether brought forward on the platform as a kind of 'tent' – does not really matter: all we are concerned with is its existence, and about that there appears to be no doubt. Fourthly, the interluders must have been familiar with those musicians' galleries which were so common in large halls, and we may suppose that they had frequently made use of them during the presentation of their plays. Hence in the construction of their theatres they carried one of the auditorium tiers across the top of the façade, thus making provision for an upper acting-area. And, lastly, since in their outdoor performances they had no doubt often suffered from the wind and the rain, they placed a half-roof over a portion of the platform. We may assume that its chief function was thus to give them protection from inclement weather, but characteristically they seized the opportunity of making it serve another purpose. Underneath, its ceiling was painted with azure sky on which appeared images of the sun, the moon, and the planets, so that in a sense Shakespeare's appropriately named Globe playhouse was made to present to the spectators a permanent emblem of the universe, with the 'heavens' above, the earth-platform and, when a trap was opened, hell underneath. Medieval symbolism was still at work.

These were the things the players did. What did they deliberately reject? The royally sponsored child-actors were making free use of painted scenery in the Franco-Italian manner: this was then the very latest thing in the theatre, and we might well have expected that the actors would have eagerly seized upon it. Yet it was precisely this for which they made no provision, and we must believe that their decision was deliberate, not fortuitous. Scenery, definitely, they did not want. Quite possibly they may have been somewhat influenced by consideration of the expense which would be incurred by the introduction of such pictorial embellishments, but that assuredly cannot have been their principal reason: they were fully prepared to lay out considerable sums for the purchase of rich attire. In the end we must believe that financial considerations weighed with them less than other considerations arising from their assessment of the public's chief interest.

This, then, was the playhouse for which Shakespeare composed his dramas, and it is the stage form which has exerted so much influence in our own theatrical endeavours. When, however, we bring it to mind either from the Elizabethan point of view or from the modern, there is one thing which must not be forgotten. If we are tempted to call it a bare stage we shall be misconceiving its function. Even although it was a magnificent platform for dramatic poetry, it was not blank and featureless; even although it was calculated to stimulate the audience's imagination, its symbolic qualities were there for all to see; and, if it had little scenic adornment, we know that the players' attire was rich and colourful. We may decide that for modern audiences a great black box, or, at the opposite extreme, a barren stage bathed in light, may be appropriate in presenting Shakespeare's tragedies; but assuredly, in doing so, we should not deceive ourselves into believing that either was the approach made to their spectators in Elizabethan times.

Thus did the Elizabethan public playhouse come into being in the year 1576, and after some ten or a dozen years had passed by it was destined to house some of the mightiest achievements in the entire range of dramatic history. So far, however, the time for such a development had not yet arrived. Indeed, a first glance at the plays produced before about 1588 might induce us to believe that the professionals' repertory was of far less significance than what was being offered by the adult amateurs and by those children of the Chapels Royal who, amateur at the start, were beginning to assume a professional status of their own. During the earlier days of the interludes none of the pieces definitely associated with the small companies appear to have so much vitality and interest as John Heywood's lively and wittily planned *Play of the Weather* (1528) or the humorous scenes which he developed in *Johan Johan* (1520) – and these, although later they were taken over by the companies of interluders, probably were penned for amateur presentation. The vast canvas of Sir David Lindsay's Scottish *Satire of the Three Estates* (1540), well known to us because of its revival at the Edinburgh Festival, is clearly to be related rather to the medieval pattern than to the Tudor. Already we have observed that, passing a few decades onward, we are apt to pause when we reach *Gorboduc*, composed, for gentlemen to perform, by two authors well acquainted with the classical Senecan model and yet not so scholarly as to prevent them from introducing the great innovation of blank verse : in a similar manner the playwrights responsible for *Ralph Roister Doister* and *Gammer Gurton's Needle* created comedies which, wider in scope than the interludes, combined liveliness in approach with a firm sense of structural form. And still more important than these efforts from within the milieu of schools, universities, and Inns of Court were those of the Chapel boys. Richard Edwards' *Damon and Pithias* (about 1565) was a remarkable drama for its time, an excellently moulded piece deliberately conceived as a tragicomedy, while, slightly later, John Lyly produced his series of prose court romances from *Campaspe* (about 1580) onward.

All of these possess historical value and one or two of them have recently been deemed worthy of at least minor revival. No great masterpieces, certainly, but with attractive and occasionally pleasurable qualities. To turn from them to the few remnants of the professionals' repertory gives us rather a shock, at least if we consider them solely for their own intrinsic virtues and not for their connections with what was to come. It would indeed be a daring and over-sanguine director who even for a moment might consider a revival of the *Excellent and pleasant Comedy, termed after the name of the Vice, Common Conditions, drawn out of the most famous history of Galiarbus, Duke of Arabia, and of the good and evil success of him and his two children, Sedmond his son, and Clarisia his daughter: set forth with delectable mirth and pleasant shews*, or of *The History of the two valiant Knights, Sir Clyomon knight of the Golden Shield, son to the King of Denmark, and Clamydes the White Knight, son to the King of Suavia*. Both must have appeared shortly after the year 1570; both may reasonably be taken as characteristic of the kind of play being cultivated by the now expanded companies; both can be regarded as possessing not the slightest inherent worth – and yet, paradoxically, if we decide to ignore them completely we shall render ourselves unable to appreciate Shakespeare's achievements properly.

The essential difference between these plays and, let us say, Lyly's comedies rests in the fact that they are deeply rooted in a folk tradition, whereas his are, in the main, idiosyncratic developments wrought out of a knowledge of classical mythology. His comedies have an atmosphere of elegance and sophistication; *Common Conditions* and *Clyomon* are rather crude exploitations of popular romance thoroughly in the style of the interludes. The Vice, as we have seen from its title, gives his name to the first play; its plot teems with adventures; there is continual mobility in it and artless variety of incident. In *Clyomon*, another Vice, called Subtle Shift, plays a similar part amid persons culled from oft-told tales; the action, starting in Suavia and Denmark, carries us far afield into a world wherein bold knights rescue distressed ladies from giant ogres and into which, somewhat to our surprise, steps in no less a person than Alexander the Great.

The dramatic material presented here shows what popular audiences were enjoying just before the establishment of The Theatre, and a third play, *The Rare Triumphs of Love and Fortune*, produced about a decade later, may be associated with the other two as indicating how the romantic subject-matter was gradually being expanded. Popular romances always introduced numerous adventures, but they also dealt largely with love and wonderment: and it is the latter path that the anonymous author of *Love and Fortune* has taken. Interestingly, he places his main action within a framework, just as Shakespeare was to do in *The Taming of the Shrew*. Here, however, there is no drunken Sly and no Lord seeking amusement: instead, we begin with a council of Olympic deities during the course of which Fortune and Venus acrimoniously quarrel with each other concerning their respective powers over mankind; and the drama itself takes shape as a kind of test demonstration of their influences, telling a story of lovers beset by obstacles and enwrapped in an atmosphere of magic.

These selected dramatic pieces, when taken together, well illustrate the movement which brought the theatre from the environment of the nobleman's hall and the village inn to that of the public stage. It is true that after 1576 the word 'interlude' is hardly ever used on a title-page as a descriptive term: for the most part it sinks to connote an old-fashioned, outworn, artificial form of entertainment – thus the artisans' 'Pyramus and Thisbe' playlet is called by that name, and in *King Lear*, when Albany makes a little moralizing speech, Goneril displays her contempt by crying out "An interlude!", just as someone today might interject "How very melodramatic!" Within the course of these few decades the professional players had moved many steps forward: their plays were longer, more intricate, and more diversified; personifications still made sporadic appearances but rapidly they were being discarded. Nevertheless, it is important to observe that the new plays, including Shakespeare's, can in no wise be seen as revolutionary. They were based ultimately upon the long interlude tradition, and within its conventions they assumed their forms. Actors, authors, and spectators were not content to be bounded by strict limitations in space and time; the public's delight came from watching variety in action with an intermingling of the serious and the comic and the wonderful. These were the forces at work in the composition of the popular plays from *Common Conditions* to *Love and Fortune*, and quite clearly the spirit of these pieces was in complete harmony with the playhouse structure deliberately adopted by the performers.

4

Elizabethan Romance and Reality

Ye rolling clouds, give Rumour room, both air and earth
  below,
By sea and land, that every ear may understand and know
What woeful hap is chancèd now within the isle of late,
Which of Strange Marshes beareth name, unto the noblest
  state.

THESE would-be serious lines, taken at random from *Clyomon and Clamydes*, may be regarded as typical of the foolishly inflated and cumbersome dialogue with which the audience's ears were battered when they crowded into The Theatre in 1576. And in scenes supposed to be comic they listened to dialogue like this:

Clyomon: Come, Knowledge, come forward. Why art thou
  always slack?
  Get you to court, brush up our apparel, untruss
  your pack.

Go seek out my page, bid him come to me with
all speed you can.

Shift: Go seek out, fetch, bring here! Gog's wounds,
what am I, a dog or a man?
I were better be a hangman, and live so like a
drudge:
Since you new man came to you, I must pack, I
must trudge!

Clyomon: How stands thou, knave? Why gets thuo not
away?

Shift: Now, now, sir, you are so hasty now, I know not
what to say.

Quite obviously, if the general spirit of these plays was in harmony with the playhouse form, the language was not.

It appears certain that the players themselves were moving forwards steadily with increasing technical skill. Before 1576 hardly any individual performers had received special commendation from their contemporaries, but very soon both tragic and comic actors were being singled out for praise: Robert Wilson was a "rare" man for his "extemporal wit", Richard Tarlton was remembered as a "famous comedian", William Kemp's "comical and conceited style" was relished, Edward Alleyn became the Roscius of the age, and laudatory comments both in prose and verse attest to the power of Richard Burbage.

Kemp, Alleyn, Burbage – with these men, of course, we have stepped over into the age of Shakespeare, and they could not have gained their eminence if their lines had contained nothing more than such stuff as is illustrated in the verses culled from *Clyomon*. Fortunately, part of the strength of the Elizabethan theatre was its adaptability. The professionals had pursued a course of their own and had succeeded in gaining for themselves an important place in the community, but they were always willing to learn. They knew that the ordinary public delighted in plays of mixed form, and consequently – much to the disgust of men like Sir Philip Sidney – they refused to chasten the expansive scope of their dramas: on the other hand, they were quite willing to admit that the amateurs' stylistic experiments offered them rich possibilities. Whereas the range of dialogue in such plays as *Clyomon and Clamydes* did not go beyond the long trailing rhymed lines called 'fourteeners' and the lines, also rhymed, of stumbling form used for the comic passages, the gentlemen amateurs had already invented the dramatic use of blank verse for serious scenes and the use of prose for comedy. And the professionals soon came to realize that these forms, partly conventional and partly realistic, were not only more effective in themselves but also capable of being employed with wider variety.

As a demonstration of what was happening in this direction hardly a better example could be found than a couple of dramas penned by the first actor-dramatist known to us, Robert Wilson. First recorded as a player in 1572, we may believe that he inherited and exploited the histrionic methods used in the early interludes; and, when he came to write *The Three Ladies of London* and its companion piece, *The Three Lords and Three Ladies of London*, we need not feel surprised to discover that both plays are, in effect, extended interludes peopled mainly by personified characters. Here, then, was a man who belonged to a vanishing tradition, and precisely because of this an examination of his dialogue yields much of interest. The first play can be dated fairly firmly about the year 1581, just five years after The Theatre had been opened, and its scenes are expressed principally in rough, stumbling couplets, slightly different from but no less crude than those in *Clyomon*. Says Simony:

> And sirrah, when I was at Rome, and dwelt in the Friary,
> They would talk how England yearly sent over a great mass of money,
> And that this little island was worth more to the Pope
> Than three bigger realms which had a great deal more scope.

Even Simplicity (presumably a part written by Wilson specially for himself) is made to speak in the same fashion:

> I knew thee when thou dwelledst at a place called Gravesend,
> And the guests knew thee too, because thou wast not their friend;
> For when thou shouldst bring reckoning to the guests,
> Thou would put twice so much, and swear it cost thy dame no less.

The second play can also be fairly firmly dated, in or about

1588. In form it does not much differ from the other, but in dialogue a great gulf stands between the two. The serious personified characters now speak in blank verse, as in Sincerity's

> Rise, Conscience, from that marble of Remorse,
> That weeping stone that scalds thy parchèd skin:
> Sincerity such robes for thee hath brought
> As best beseems good Conscience to adorn;

and the change in Simplicity's utterance is positively startling:

> A score, wife? You mean for the alehouse, do you not? (*aside, to the audience*) I would have her examine me thereof no further, for I am in too far there, more than I would she should know.

The important thing to observe here is that, although the style of neither play has any real distinction, nothing could be made from the former whereas the latter has vast potentialities: all that was needed was for a distinguished poet to come and give it vigour, intensity, and beauty, and for other authors to give it diversified range.

Everyone knows that the blazoning standard of the new movement was boldly unfurled when, at the first performance of Christopher Marlowe's *Tamburlaine,* about 1588, the audience was startled and exhilarated by the few emphatic lines delivered by the prologue-speaker:

> From jigging veins of riming mother-wits
> And such conceits as clownage keeps in pay,
> We'll lead you to the stately tents of war,
> Where you shall hear the Scythian Tamburlaine
> Threatening the world in high-astounding terms.

In wonderment they listened to the fulfilment of this boast, conscious of the fact that nothing so rich and so exciting had previously been heard upon the stage. An unprecedented age of drama had begun.

If, however, Marlowe had stood alone, perhaps even if his life had not been suddenly and squalidly ended in a Deptford tavern brawl, it is unlikely that the later Elizabethan theatre would have exhibited its passionate vitality or that the young William Shakespeare would so easily and so rapidly have moved from apprenticeship to maturity. Marlowe was master of high-astounding terms, certainly; but his aggressive spirit was not well qualified to express the ordinary – and dramas tend to become dull when they are all sounded on a single note. To a large degree, also, the very forcefulness of his own character restricted his power as a dramatist: a poet of genius, free-thinking and gifted with wide vision, he tended to reach his most effective scenes rather by projecting himself into his fictional persons than by giving to these persons vital characteristics of their own. His achievement was great: his *Tamburlaine*, *Dr Faustus*, *The Jew of Malta*, and *Edward II* are the first plays in the history of the English drama which can unreservedly be regarded as works worthy of minute examination. Yet we must be honest with ourselves; and, if we are strictly honest, we are bound to admit that 'reading' and not 'witnessing' is the appropriate word. These plays can still be revived occasionally on the stage with interest, and sometimes the revivals, by the skill of directors and actors, have been made truly impressive. On the other hand, the scanning of the poet's lines on the printed page generally yields a much more powerful vision than is produced by any stage action. The concept of *Dr Faustus* is powerful, but its deepest impact comes from the creation within a reader's mind of an imaginary ambience: we may see on the boards a Helen impersonated by what the public regards as the most beautiful living actress and listen to Faust's invocation delivered by a prominent actor – and still feel dissatisfied because the vision and the glorious lines are cast in freely poetic and not in dramatically poetic mould. Although all credit must be given to Marlowe as an innovator, in so far as the drama was concerned much more was needed to supplement his efforts.

In fact, the sudden expansion of the theatre during the last years of Queen Elizabeth's reign was due to the strange fact that within half a dozen years from about 1587 to about 1595 numerous other playwrights, including the young Shakespeare, all working within the same general stylistic form, made their own distinctly individual contributions to a common treasury. There is no space in a brief survey such as the present to list and analyse the separate offerings to the playhouse made by all these men – Thomas Kyd, George Peele, and their companions; but one single example may be selected to serve as a typical illustration. Among these writers not least interesting was poor Robert Greene, even although he was not able to leave behind him anything so startling and so impressive as Marlowe had done. Like most of his fellows, he was greatly influenced by such plays as *Tamburlaine* and *Dr Faustus*, but his nature was not framed in the Marlovian mould: a roisterer who ended his life miserably in abject poverty, his imagination was richer in visions of quiet rustic things than in symbols of soaring ambition. Thus in his *Friar Bacon and Friar Bungay* (about 1589) he could depart from the terrible despair of Faust's study and open his play amid the country delights of Fressingfield fair, introducing therein what Marlowe had failed to produce, a charming portrait of an ordinary simple heroine. How he accomplished this deserves a moment's attention. His Margaret is first put before us in the company of a farm-servant Thomas, whose prose speech succeeds at once in giving him his proper character:

> By my troth, Margaret, here's a weather is able to make a man call his father whoreson. If this weather hold, we shall have hay good cheap, and butter and cheese at Harlston will bear no price.

Margaret is only a farmer's daughter, not one born to noble estate, but Greene makes her reply to Thomas in the blank-verse measure which had come to be reserved generally for the upper-class, better-educated, and serious dramatic characters:

> Thomas, maids when they come to see the fair
> Count not to make a cope for dearth of hay.
> When we have turn'd our butter to the salt,
> And set our cheese safely upon the racks,
> Then let our fathers price it as they please.
> We country sluts of merry Fressingfield
> Come to buy needless naughts to make us fine,
> And look that young men should be frank this day
> And court us with such fairings as they can.

Two things call for attention here. This first speech in which his heroine is presented to us has been given by Greene a bold, emphatic alliterative quality, of a kind likely to catch the audience's ears: he wants them to give particular heed to the lines, and he captures the public by the very sound of his words.

Secondly, the blank verse which he gives to Margaret is wrought in such a way as to adjust it to her situation. There are no high-astounding terms here; the music of the lines may be rich, but the words she uses are homely, almost as rustic as those put into Thomas' mouth – 'dearth of hay', 'butter', 'salt', 'cheese', 'needless naughts', 'fairings'. Thus is she set firmly before us, just a farmer's daughter who can converse on equal terms with a country clown, and yet a girl gifted with something more than a pretty face: the fact that Greene gives her blank verse to speak on her first entrance not only sets her apart from Thomas, but also allows him to make her language soar when, later in the play, her passions are aroused: rejecting an illicit proposal made to her by the Prince of Wales, her contemptuous words,

Why, thinks King Henry's son that Margaret's love
Hangs in the uncertain balance of proud time?

are set on a level far beyond her earlier utterances, and yet at the same time are in perfect harmony with them.

These two lines suggest a further reflection. If the play of *Friar Bacon and Friar Bungay* had been lost, and if Margaret's proud question had alone been preserved, anonymously, in some sixteenth-century commonplace-book, might we not easily have been led to believe that their melody and colour pointed to Shakespeare's authorship? The clear fact is that all these writers, Shakespeare included, were working towards the development of a general dramatic style. Naturally, they differed in power, but the two-fold truth has to be fully appreciated – that, on the one hand, Shakespeare belonged to the prevailing tradition dominant in his age, and, on the other, that even lesser writers could on occasion rise momentarily to his height. The tradition, moreover, was not simply one which had been established by a single author and followed by others: it was through the combined efforts of many men that the theatre, within the space of only a few years, found itself possessed of a form of expression richer even than that possessed by the Athenians during their all-too-brief days of consummate glory.

This universal, supple, and effective range in style was eagerly exploited by the professional players: they had made themselves into excellent instrumentalists, and now they were being offered verbal compositions worthy of their talents. And at the same time they and the dramatists they employed were alert to take advantage of a corresponding development in structural form. In considering this, however, we have to tread somewhat warily, if we are to understand aright what was happening.

The amateurs, as we have seen, even although they often exhibited an attractive independence, tended in general to look back to classical models: occasionally scenes of laughter might be mingled with serious episodes, but usually the tragic and the comic were kept separate and apart; the examples of the Roman Seneca, Terence, and Plautus remained ever in mind. The professional players and playwrights, on the other hand, had learned from their experience that the public was attracted most by adventuresome, hybrid story plays, with the subject-matter taken sometimes from narrative romances and sometimes from tales of ancient monarchs such as the Persian Cambyses and Darius. Since these dramas commonly mingled together characters and episodes of varying kinds, with the comic scenes jostling the serious, they usually had no firm architectural shape: all that mattered was the telling of the story and keeping the spectators amused by any means that came to hand.

As the drama expanded after the establishment of The Theatre, however, the professionals evidently became aware of the virtues inherent in the more disciplined amateur approach, but even at this stage we should think less of any taking over of classical forms than of a gradual development of a sense of form which might be applied to the structure of plays romantic-ally conceived. It is true that after about 1587 'tragedies' came to be part of the professional repertory, yet it is clear that the period from then on to 1600 did not find its most characteristic expression in the tragic style and that the majority of such tragedies as were produced refused to be bound by classical restraint. The architectural planning of *Tamburlaine* is expan-sive, and there is reason to believe that originally it included some comic material — "fond and frivolous gestures", which were omitted from the printed text; the hero of *Dr Faustus* was obviously outside the princely character range which classically-minded critics deemed proper to the tragic style;

Thomas Kyd's popular *Spanish Tragedy* was thoroughly romantic in structure; the anonymous author of *Arden of Feversham* boldly broke with all ancient tradition by dealing with ordinary middle-class persons amid humble surroundings; and even *Romeo and Juliet*, despite its pair of star-crossed lovers, may be thought to have more spiritual communion with *Much Ado about Nothing* than with *Othello* or *King Lear*.

All of this may be put in another way by saying that when these men did essay the tragic style they shaped the style itself in conformity with the tradition to which they were accustomed. Much more commonly they built on the foundation of their plays of mixed form, the adventuresome stories of romance and historical events, investing these with a fresh shaping image which served to bind the diversified material into complex dramatically artistic patterns – producing thus not merely the most characteristic but also the most excitingly enduring achievements of the late-sixteenth-century theatre.

Shakespeare's long series of chronicle-histories, with the exception of *King Henry VIII*, all come from this time, and, in view of their many recent revivals, it is very important to consider carefully the kind of vision which inspired their composition. During the past few years several critical studies and a number of stage productions have tended to emphasize their grimness and their exhibition of the grinding "mechanism of history". For this approach considerable justification may be found; our attention needs to be drawn to the vigorous and unsentimental historical picture here set up before us; yet the approach itself, if made too emphatic, may be thought to result in a simplification of what these plays reveal and consequently in a lessening of their worth for us. Let us at least consider this possibility.

If *King John* and *King Henry VIII* are left out of account we are concerned with eight plays, and for their assessment we have to recognize the existence of two conflicts; the first is that between the individual dramas and the series as a whole, a conflict made more complex because *King Henry VI* is shaped as a three-part work while *King Henry IV* is two-part; the second is that between two chronological patterns, the actual and the theatrical. The actual historical scheme takes us from the murder of Richard II, in 1400, through the reigns of

Henry IV (1399–1413), Henry V (1413–22), and Henry VI (1422–61 and, later, 1470–71), on to that of Richard III (1483–85). When, however, we turn to the order in which the various plays were written the sequence is entirely different. In his early apprentice days, probably between 1590 and 1592, Shakespeare composed *King Henry VI* in a manner which truly agrees with the significance of the term 'chronicle-history', making it a condensed record of the torments and tensions of that King's reign; shortly afterwards, in the highly theatrical *King Richard III*, he concentrated on one terrible central figure, granting him just such vigour and just such sardonic humour as might win audience interest in his personality; in his next contribution to the series, probably in 1595, he turned back to the beginning in *King Richard II*, moulding this play so that it became a study in two contrasting characters and, at the same time, a kind of symbolic opening to the long years of strife which he was engaged in dramatizing; then, after the lapse of at least two years, he applied himself, in the maturity of his artistic life, to the reigns of Henry IV and his son, widening his range and enriching the chronicle pattern with his own inventions.

Now, it seems incontrovertible that as he progressed Shakespeare was gradually feeling his way towards something only dimly conceived at the start: *King Henry IV* and, in spite of its chauvinism, *King Henry V* are shaped in a form profounder in import and more varied in design than the others; in them the dramatist appears to have been saying his last word on the series of events on which his imagination had been playing during the course of almost a full decade. In them dark reflections are by no means absent, and inexorably history continues on its haggard path; yet in these three latest dramas we are carried further, laughter sounding amidst the metallic clash of arms. And this laughter is of various sorts. Falstaff's wit, associated with the disreputable crew with whom, ambling and strutting, he consorts, arouses one of these, and in listening to his words we realize that in essence this great comic creation derives ultimately from the popular Vice of the interludes: the Vice always had to be rejected in the end, yet in his merriment the audience had richly shared. Another kind of laughter comes when Shakespeare invents his Gower, Fluellen, and

Macmorris, the laughter that arises from the clash of personalities among a group of friends. And a third ripples in a girl's
jollity, as she, acquainted only with her native French,
hurriedly tries to learn a few English words and, with eyes dancing and yet a little apprehensive, is confronted by her blunt
Petruchio-Hal.

Our interpretation of these dramas must, it would seem,
include everything : nothing must be suppressed. May it not be
thought that the recent tendency to set their action within a
milieu reminiscent of that of *Mother Courage* has the effect of
reducing and lessening Shakespeare's total and mature vision?
May not this trend towards concentrating upon the cruel and
the bloodily grim be considered as being, in fact, no less false
than the older fashion of glozing over the scenes of horror?
In trying to assess the quality of these plays do we not have to
remember that, as Shakespeare perfected his art, he deliberately chose as rich and variegated a design as he could imagine,
wherein the ominous threats and sanguinary actions are inter-
meshed with laughter wittily vulgar, honestly deep, and charm-
ingly feminine?

It was not, of course, only Shakespeare who eagerly exploited historical subject-matter. George Peele dealt with *King
Edward I*, Marlowe with *King Edward II*, an unknown
author or authors with *King Edward III*, and probably another play of unknown authorship, *Thomas of Woodstock*,
dealing with the first years of Richard II's reign, was known
to Shakespeare before he applied himself to the task of narrat-
ing that monarch's last tragic days. Within this realm the
Elizabethans, Shakespeare and his companions, found scope
more fruitful than they could in the more restricted sphere of
classically inspired tragedy; and equally fertile soil did they find
in the area of romance. That these two styles of drama were
intimately related is shown immediately by the fact that, apart
from the many plays which attempted to deal seriously with
historical subject-matter, in numerous others historical events,
freely coloured by the fancy, were associated with themes and
characters culled from romances and folklore.   Greene's
Scottish History of James IV is by no means a chronicle-play
like the others: its story is invented, and it starts with Oberam,
King of the Fairies. The two parts of *Robert, Earl of Hunting-*

don, written by Henry Chettle and Anthony Munday, although placed in a quasi-historical setting, deal with the adventures of Robin Hood in his greenwood retreat – and there is significance in the probability that the success of these plays, produced in 1598 by the Admiral's Men, was responsible for stimulating Shakespeare into composing his own rival greenwood romantic comedy, appropriately called *As You Like It*.

In such works poets, players, and public all delighted. Here elements diverse and often apparently contradictory could be made to harmonize: the firm, the ordinary, the palpable could stand alongside the airy, the wondrous, the fantastical; here mortals and creatures supernatural could meet and converse; dreaming and waking could become hardly distinguishable. At the very start of his career Shakespeare made up his *Comedy of Errors* from two plays written by Plautus, but what he did to the Plautan material resulted in an entirely different kind of drama. He expanded the adventures of the various characters; he set his action in Ephesus, but made this antique city embrace a nunnery within its walls; the abbess is Æmilia, wife to Ægeon; the wooing of Luciana is romantic, not Roman; as the perplexed men and women move within their net of errors it seems to them that Ephesus is instinct with magic and they wonder whether they dream or wake.

This romantic world is one of wonder. Greene's *Friar Bacon and Friar Bungay*, which had started in the familiar countryside of merry Fressingfield, soon moves into the charmed surroundings of Bacon's study, where we see persons mysteriously rapt through the air, where we encounter a marvellous glass which, like an anticipation of closed-circuit television, shows images of persons walking and conversing many miles away, where we look upon a brazen head which might equally be counted an anticipation of modern man's computers. True, this last magical device breaks down: but are there no computer failures? In Shakespeare's *A Midsummer Night's Dream* an antique Theseus and an Amazonian Hippolyta, inhabiting a realm half-historical, half-legendary, co-exist not only with the Elizabethan company of Bottom and Quince but also with the magic-working creatures who haunt the recesses of the forest. Here the 'rare triumphs' of *Love and Fortune*, with its perplexed lovers and its magician Bomelio, are made rarer and still more triumphant.

The world of romance thus put upon the stage is intricate in its variety, and it would appear that an appreciation of what it has to offer us can be gained only through an understanding of its delicate balance. If we go to extremes, stressing one element at the expense of others, imposing alien patterns of our own, its essential quality vanishes immediately. Thus, for instance, we must see that these plays were not simply things of joy and careless happiness. Sadness often intrudes; hardly a single one of Shakespeare's comedies is without the thought of death; amid the present laughter there is the image of time's bending sickle; the fairies in *A Midsummer Night's Dream* are delightful, but they can also be menacing, and their ruler is specifically named a King of the Shadows. This darker element, like the grimness inherent in the history plays, has lately attracted the attention of some critics and directors who, by underlining its force, have turned dream into nightmare. In doing so they have rightly reacted against Victorian sentimentalism; yet the casting-out of Mendelssohn's musical accompaniment and the substitution of modern discords hardly lead us closer towards a grasping of Shakespeare's complete vision.

Some other directors have inclined towards the opposite extreme, treating *A Midsummer Night's Dream* as a kind of burlesque 'Western' and *Much Ado about Nothing* as though it were a cheap Sicilian farce. No doubt such productions become raucously laughable, and if we consider them simply as shows they can be accepted. On the other hand, Shakespeare was manifestly an artist of almost unrivalled subtlety and we must admit that in productions of this kind something different, less profound, and therefore by far less meaningful is being presented to us. If a balance is preserved the hints of malice, the sense of time's inexorable tread, the threats of pain acquire a stronger and more suggestive force than they do when they are overstressed; and something indeed is wrong when, in a farcical presentation of *Much Ado about Nothing*, the excess of ridiculous business which has kept us laughing from the very start of the play suddenly has the effect of making Dogberry's luscious scenes appear to be singularly unamusing.

There would seem, then, to be no doubt that the quality

inherent in these romantic comedies depends upon their complexity, a complexity which can mean as much to us as assuredly it did to the spectators for whom they were originally conceived. And here, in endeavouring to appreciate its potency, it may be well to examine a particular dramatic invention of the period which was intimately characteristic of its spirit. Already we have observed that in the old play of *Love and Fortune* the story of the lovers and Bomelio was enclosed within the story of Jove and his fellow-deities – and just such a device, in various forms, appears in numerous plays of the succeeding years. Oberam 'presents' the main action of Greene's *James IV*; Venus introduces the play of *Alphonsus*; a Ghost and the personified figure of Revenge watch the scenes of *The Spanish Tragedy*, just as the story of *Soliman and Perseda* is watched by Love, Death, and Fortune; *The Taming of the Shrew* is enacted by a group of fictional players before a Lord and Christopher Sly, who of course are themselves actors; in *Robert, Earl of Huntingdon* the far-off, fabulous adventures of Robin Hood are complicated, and enriched, by the fact that the audience is led to believe that these are being interpreted by amateur and other performers living in the period of Henry VIII.

At first, perhaps, we might be tempted to dismiss all such examples as no more than mere repetitions of a dramatic trick; but further consideration must make us pause. In the first place, we realize that the device itself is thoroughly consonant with the architectural form assumed by the Elizabethan theatre. The actors who, after having taken their parts in the introductory scene, sit down to watch the action within an action, take their places in the gallery alongside members of the public, thus forming a bridge between the auditorium and the stage. And, even more significantly, the device is seen to be admirably concordant with the entire fabric of the romantic drama – deities and creatures of the folk imagination may thus envelope what purports to be the real, or the purportedly real may envelope the fantastic. Thirdly, when we relate the device itself to the long-enduring disguise element so freely exploited in the interludes, we realize that both, taken in conjunction, combine to produce that constant interplay of appearance and reality which forms the inner core of this imaginative entity. To appreciate the spirit thus invoked, we need do no more than examine briefly a single example. *The Taming of the Shrew* is not one of Shakespeare's most profound inventions, and it may all too readily be set aside as a mere farce. Let us, however, try to think of the effect it must have produced on those who were privileged to witness its first performances.

At the start the spectators see a very familiar scene – a sodden drunk being chucked out of a tavern: there he lies on the stage as he might have lain on a muddy roadway. Then they hear the equally familiar sound of a huntsman's horn, and in comes a recognizably real Elizabethan lord attended by his servitors: despite the fact that he speaks, according to the accepted convention, in blank verse, the spectators feel that they are still watching and listening to something which is a direct image of the matter-of-fact world which they themselves inhabit. They continue so to watch and listen when they move to the second scene: they are now taken into the Lord's mansion, where the inebriated Sly wakens up on a luxurious bed and, surrounded by things and persons strange to him, is at least half-persuaded that he is truly a lord, that the 'real' Christopher Sly, the drunken sot, had been nothing save a bad dream. Already, therefore, the contrast between appearance and reality is thematically introduced into what is merely the enveloping action. Then the 'real' Lord, whom the audience know to be interpreted by an actor, calls into service a group of performers – and at once the whole movement of the comedy is carried onto another plane. These performers pretend they are fictional characters living in distant Italy, but very soon the spectators, watching the fortunes of Petruchio and his Kate, are tending to accept the twice-removed persons as the real. Within the course of this inner play, moreover, there soon appear inner circles of their own. One character puts on a disguise through which the audience instantly penetrates but which deceives at least some of his companions; the audience knows that Petruchio, despite his extravagant behaviour, is not the callous, brutal boor he seems to others on the stage; while even the spectators are agreeably cheated when they come to realize that Kate has been won, not so much by her husband's stern treatment, as by the very simple fact that she has, perhaps without her knowing it, been in love with him from the beginning. In the scene of the sun and the moon, when they meet the old man on the road, she truly becomes the merry Kate who is the fitting companion and match for Petruchio. There is even some justification for interpreting her final speech, not crudely but delicately, as a sort of elaborate parody, uttered with such conscious and contrived exaggeration as to leave the poor man in wonderment, vaguely disturbed lest he should have found himself hoist with his own petard. And if we assume, as no doubt we must, that the original text of Shakespeare's play had an epilogue to correspond with its opening scenic prologue, still another circle is shaped for us. Sly, once more snoring in a drunken stupor, is carried by the Lord's servants to the muddy roadside from which they picked him up: waking, he remembers both the reality and the dream – or ought we to say, the dream and the reality – the two overlapping, coalescing, merging into each other.

The importance of endeavouring to place ourselves in the position of the spectators who first saw this play seems self-evident. For them the dress of Sly and the Lord and the servants was the same as that in which they themselves were attired, and the covention of verse speech was so common that it could be accepted without question; for us these characters are clad in strange theatrical garments, and consequently we inevitably lose a large part of the original effect; while the language spoken, even although we are fairly well accustomed to it from our attendance at performances of Shakespearian plays, obviously cannot produce the same impression as it unquestionably did in Elizabethan times – partly because the convention is no longer our own, and partly because the correlation between the blank-verse form and the common speech of those days is different from that between the poetic tones and the harsher, commoner speech of our age. Despite this, however, only a slight effort of the imagination is called for in order to appreciate the subtlety of Shakespeare's patterning of the play.

The play itself, as we all know, is after all mainly a comedy farce, and consequently the planes of reality which are presented in it are by no means so intricate as those to be traced in Shakespeare's more mature romantic comedies – although maybe their comparative crudity in presentation serves the better to demonstrate the harmony between this characteristic dramatic form and the architectural shape of the Elizabethan playhouse. We inhabit a world here of converging circles in which the action of the play is both brought close to the audience and yet distanced from them. And in its ultimate reach it can proceed beyond the very bounds of the theatre and attain to a metaphysical vision, the kind of vision supremely revealed in *The Tempest*. It is true that this romance was one of Shakespeare's latest works, written almost a decade after Queen Elizabeth's death, yet it belongs in spirit to an earlier time: unquestionably it was created out of what may be styled the strictly Elizabethan experience. Here, sitting in the Globe theatre, the public found themselves carried off to a distant magical island, where the 'real', from the coarseness of Trinculo to the refined evil of Antonio and Sebastian and the honest garrulity of Gonzalo, could co-exist with an evanescent Ariel and a Caliban half human, half diabolic. In order to delight Miranda and her newly discovered Ferdinand the magic-working Prospero has summoned his attendant spirits to present an allegorical masque. Iris, Juno, and Ceres have come to bless the union of the lovers: the Nymphs are there, and Iris summons fit companions for them:

> You sun-burnt sicklemen, of August weary,
> Come hither from the furrow, and be merry;
> Make holiday; your rye-straw hats put on,
> And these fresh nymphs encounter every one
> In country footing.

Then, suddenly recalling the foul conspiracy plotted against him by the Caliban crew, Prospero causes them to vanish. Ferdinand rises in confusion, and the magician is given an opportunity of uttering his most famous and most penetrating speech. "You do look, my son," he says

> in a mov'd sort,
> As if you were dismay'd. Be cheerful, sir;
> Our revels now are ended. These our actors,
> As I foretold you, were all spirits, and
> Are melted into air —

and then, as though he himself becomes rapt in his own mystical imaginative concept, he moves from the particular to the general —

– into thin air,
And, like the baseless fabric of this vision,
The cloud-capp'd towers, the gorgeous palaces,
The solemn temples, the great globe itself,
Yea, all which it inherit, shall dissolve,
And, like this insubstantial pageant, faded,
Leave not a rack behind.

At this moment, as if he were become conscious of indulging in grandiloquent preaching, he descends to earth with words of simpler – and for that very reason, of even more impressive – force:

We are such stuff
As dreams are made on; and our little life
Is rounded with a sleep.

The words are among the best-known in the whole of Shakespeare's writings, and in them, we might justifiably declare, is to be discerned the supreme and the ultimate expression of the spirit animating the Elizabethan theatre. Whether we share the vision, whether we like it or not, herein rests that theatre's symbol or emblem. In Prospero's speech all has been summed up; and beyond it, on such a path, it is impossible to go.

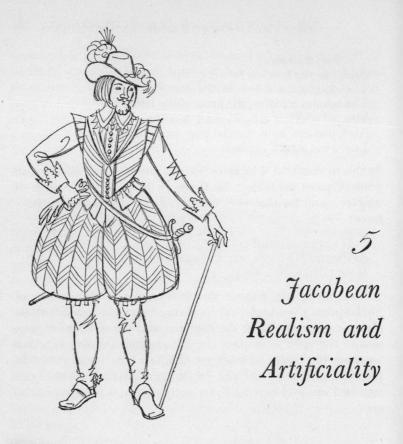

5

Jacobean Realism and Artificiality

JUST about six hundred years separated the first liturgical playlets from Marlowe's *Tamburlaine*; but whereas the medieval world had moved with slow, leisurely pace, the era which gave birth to the poetic vision of the Scythian conqueror was one of rapid and sometimes violent movement. Hardly two decades had passed by before there arose a new dramatic movement so unexpectedly like the new movement in our own times as to demand very particular examination.

Sudden, certainly, was the advent of this *avant-garde* development, datable almost as precisely as that which came like a spate after the production, in 1956, of John Osborne's *Look Back in Anger*. And this flood, too, was one which expressed itself alike in general social terms, in experimentation with novel dramatic forms, and in the cultivation of a fresh kind of theatre structure.

Perhaps it may be best to begin with the last of these, since consideration of theatrical activities during the early years of the seventeenth century offers an interesting and at the same time a paradoxical connection with stage activities in our own period. We all know that, during recent decades, the 'open stage', largely inspired by the rediscovery of Shakespeare's Globe playhouse, has become the ruling fashion: the older proscenium-arch theatres necessarily are still being used, but constant endeavour is being made to push the acting-area inwards towards the audience and so to break the hard rigours of the curtain-line, while, concurrently, newly built theatres – such as that at Chichester – are designed so as to dispense with the proscenium-arch entirely. The paradox which becomes evident when we relate this new modern movement with the new movement which started at the very end of Queen Elizabeth's reign is that, while the revolutionary young dramatists and theatre-men of her age were equally inspired by a desire to cultivate a novel playhouse form, they proceeded, as it were, in a reverse direction. For them the open stage was old-fashioned, and in effect they moved, in their revolt, towards what now has become to our way of thinking an old-fashioned style in theatre architecture.

It was in 1599 that the child-actors, the little eyases so bitingly castigated in *Hamlet*, inexplicably caught the attention of the fashionable public in London, presenting their plays in an indoor structure at Blackfriars which, if it did not have exactly the proportions and arrangements of a nineteenth-century proscenium-arch theatre, even if it cultivated most of the techniques familiar on the open platform of the Globe, was clearly pointing the way forward towards something different. It is true that, when the old Globe was burned to the ground in 1613, Shakespeare's company immediately proceeded to erect another Globe to take its place; it is also true that the Fortune of 1600 and the Red Bull of 1605 were constructed on the old open-air plan; but against these facts must be put, first, the fact that the King's Men found themselves compelled, about 1609, to take over the Blackfriars as an additional – and, it would appear, an increasingly important – theatrical home, and, secondly, the fact that the essentially characteristic playhouses built during the earlier part of the seventeenth century – the

Phoenix, or Cockpit, of 1616, and the Salisbury Court theatre of 1629 – were indoor houses. Everyone was aware of the distinction between the two types: the older model, typified in the Globe, came to be called the 'public' playhouse, and the newer model, precisely because it was a closed-in structure, was styled the 'private' house.

It can no more be asserted that the novel styles in drama were exclusively developed within these new theatres than it can be said that our own *avant-garde* plays all belong to the open-stages which have now become popular: several of the young innovators started their apprenticeship on the boards well trodden by their predecessors, and some of them proceeded to pen works both for the fashionable children's companies and for the adult professional players. Nevertheless, an examination of the dramas written for the new so-called 'private' houses and those designed for production on the so-called 'public' stages unmistakably indicates that the two tended to be different in spirit, tone, and, sometimes, texture. We may well believe that this difference is ultimately to be traced back to the difference between the widely representative general audience variously placed within the sweeping walls of the Globe and the more limited, intellectual, and probably youthful body of spectators seated on the benches within the more restricted, enclosed area of the Blackfriars. With the establishment of the private houses, what had once been a realm of general entertainment, welcoming all and sundry from courtiers to carters, was inclining to become sectionalized, so that within a few years such a theatre as the Red Bull could be superiorly laughed at as the haunt of the ignorant, the vulgar, and the common, while the Cockpit could reasonably expect its patrons to be mostly an assemblage of gentlemen and their assorted ladies.

In this development, too, another connection and paradox becomes apparent. In both periods, the modern and the seventeenth-century Jacobean, the new drama has tended to appeal to younger intellectuals, yet whereas ours has for the most part sprung from the disgruntled emotions of Jimmy Porters with social chips on their shoulders, the other arose from within the world of the *élite*, the well-born if sometimes impecunious sons of established families, the university men, the minor courtiers, the denizens of the Inns of Court.

What was the particular spark which fired off the new movement is difficult to determine, but one thing is certain – during the last year of the sixteenth century and the first year of the seventeenth a fresh style makes its appearance in various guises. Outside of the specifically theatrical realm, epigrammatically satirical and occasionally libellous verses start to circulate so freely that the authorities deem it necessary to impose a rigorous censorship: numerous young writers, among them Marston and Tourneur, begin to cultivate personal and private, often grotesque, stylistic forms, penning lines which presumably could yield meanings only to themselves or to intimate initiates. Tourneur, for example, in a long incomprehensible poem called *The Transformed Metamorphosis,* published in 1600, can write stanzas such as:

> What dreadful sight (O) do mine eyes behold?
> See frosty age, that should direct aright
> The grassy brain (that is in vice so bold)
> With heedy doctrine and celestial light,
> Hath been conversing with hell's taper, night,
> Whose devilish charms, like Circe's sorcery,
> Have metamorphosed Eos' Eonie –

or

> O who persuades my willing errorie
> Into this black chimerianized night?
> Who leads me into this concavity,
> This huge concavity, defect of light,
> To feel the smart of Phlegetontic sight?
> O who, I say, persuades mine infant eye
> To gaze upon my youth's obscurity?

Amid the incomprehensibility one thing seems to be clear: the deliberately crabbed verse and the monstrous vocabulary are the result of a desire to be 'different' and, in particular, to convince the author (if nobody else) that he belongs to a small body of the elect. The mood thus expressed had, in fact, been anticipated a few years before by George Chapman, a poet who ever sought to condemn the popular and all its delights. Where this led him is clearly shown in his obscure poem *The Shadow of Night*: observing that ordinary men love the sun's radiance, he can think of nothing else save the giving of praise to the darkness of night, when, he emphasizes, such choice souls as himself could contemplate in isolation from the vulgar snoring commonalty. Contemporary puritans were not the only men who found satisfaction in belonging to a small, self-chosen body of predestinates.

Within the theatre, as we have already seen, Marston gave expression to the new mood in his *Antonio and Mellida*, while only a few months earlier the aggressive Ben Jonson presented his first important play, *Every Man in his Humour*, thus launching the vogue of social satire on the stage. True, the earliest form of this latter play was different from that which later was printed in Jonson's collected works, and we cannot be quite sure in what year its self-confident prologue was composed; but we may be sure that the ideas enunciated in that prologue were already well developed in the author's mind. If we care to consider this prologue alongside Shakespeare's introduction to *Henry V* we may secure a vivid sense of the distinction between the old mode and the new, and, in addition, an appreciation of the completely variant approaches of the two dramatists. 'Gentle' Shakespeare addresses the spectators as 'gentles', humbly apologizes for the 'imperfections' of himself and his fellow-actors, and, above all, stresses that everything must depend upon the audience's imaginative powers. The whole spirit of these lines is instinct with wise magnanimity. By contrast, Jonson begins with ridicule of the romantic absurdities which ruled the stage and, by implication, demonstrates his contempt for the public which had been prepared to find pleasure in such follies : he is neither gentle himself nor does he treat his public as such. The vast expanse of the romantic theatre is castigated, not only the comedies but also the chronicle histories which had dealt, by means of

> three rusty swords,
> And help of some few foot-and-half-foot words,

with "York and Lancaster's long wars". Then, in a manner of absolute assurance, he confidently proclaims that in his masterpiece the spectators will have the privilege of witnessing a drama such as other plays ought to be, containing

deeds and language such as men do use,
And persons such as Comedy would choose,
When she would show an image of the times.

The way is clearly being set for the realistic stage, for the angry
young men, for the intellectual theatre, for a complete change
in attitudes. During the last years of the sixteenth century there
had, of course, been some 'realistic' plays, both serious and
comic: already reference has been made to the domestic
'tragedy' of *Arden of Feversham*, and there were others of a
similar kind; but the great mass of serious dramas were set in
distant times and far-off places. And comedy disported herself
most happily in realms of the fancy: not a single Shakespearian
comic play is set in contemporary London, and here the master
followed the same path as his fellows; even those few who, like
Henry Porter with his *Two Angry Women of Abingdon* (about
1589) and Thomas Dekker with his delightfully charming
Shoemakers' Holiday (1599), deal with ordinary English
characters in their own familiar surroundings generally chose
to move out of the city into the countryside or else to distance
their scenes by placing the action in the past. Nor should it be
assumed that Jonson's strictures suddenly banished all the typical Elizabethan styles from the boards. Chronicle-histories, it
is true, are less numerous after the turn of the century, but that
must have been largely due to the fact that the more interesting reigns had already been recorded in stage form: and certainly sufficient interest in the form remained to induce several
authors, after Elizabeth's death, to deal with events which could
not have been handled during her lifetime – Dekker thus
treated the unhappy story of Lady Jane Grey in his *Sir Thomas
Wyatt* (1604), during the same year Samuel Rowley's *When
You See Me You Know Me* seized upon the reign of Henry
VIII, and Heywood's *If You Know Not Me You Know Nobody* narrated within its two parts the troubles and triumphs of
the great Queen herself, while in 1613 Shakespeare's last play
was *King Henry VIII*. At the same time romantic comedies
planned in accordance with earlier styles continued to please
popular audiences, and the old expansiveness still endured. We
have only to glance at the numerous plays written by Dekker
and Heywood to realize the persisting force of the Elizabethan
inspiration.

Despite all of this, however, the first decade and a half of the seventeenth century was most strongly marked by the vogue of two kinds of play – satirical comedy, sometimes almost farcical, sometimes bitter, occasionally general in scope but more often personal – and what can be called only the theatre of disgust. Over the former of these two realms Ben Jonson presided, descending to the expression of personal animosities in *Cynthia's Revels* (1601), achieving a richer and broader comic canvas in *Bartholomew Fair* (1614) and *The Alchemist* (1610), losing himself in the sardonic and tormented pattern of evil set forth in *Volpone* (1606). Concerning Jonson's genius there is no doubt, nor can there be any doubt concerning his abiding influence. Within his own lifetime he was the master of a school of playwrights who, the adopted 'sons' of Ben, followed his lead, and the stamp of his comic style can be traced well on into the eighteenth century: indeed, there were many men of the theatre prepared to place him in a niche above that occupied by Shakespeare. When this has been fully admitted, however, it is still necessary to observe that essentially he was a dramatist of an age, and not of all time] In striving to exhibit the deeds and language that men do use, he unquestionably

succeeded in reproducing the tones of his own period, but, in doing so, he tended to lose sight of the eternal through the attention he paid to the temporary. Contemporary follies and vices are made to tread the boards in his plays, yet rarely do we sense in his works any true constructive social purpose, any ideas concerning the way in which society might be bettered. In his aggressive, self-satisfied assurance he angrily castigates what seems to him stupid, but his anger generally springs from a sense of his own personal superiority. Although the image of grasping, savagely clawing beasts and birds of prey gives to *Volpone* something of an inverted magnificence, the mordant comedy fails to yield its full impact in the theatre precisely because it lacks balance and contrast. When we read its text on the printed page its powerful strength is evident; when we witness its scenes on the stage it is apt to leave us dissatisfied.

In *Volpone* there are elements both grotesque and cruel; and, even although Jonson wrote nothing remotely akin to *Antonio and Mellida*, it is by no means surprising to find him associated, in the writing of *Eastward Ho* (1605), both with

Marston and with Chapman. These three authors, with their lack of counterpoise and contrast and with their anger and disgust largely limited by personal interests, express a mood which characterizes most of the *avant-garde* plays composed during those years: *Antonio and Mellida* deals with 'tragic' events and becomes a comedy of the absurd; and *Volpone*, technically a comedy, approaches close to the spirit of the theatre of cruelty.

In this connection a rapid glance at the play titles popular during those years is neither uninteresting nor uninstructive. Fashions in the names given to dramas at different periods are often as distinctive as the clothes which we know their authors wore, so much so indeed that often, given the mere title of a play, we can guess its approximate date with almost as much assurance as we can estimate the date of a portrait by looking at the suit worn by the sitter. Still further, just as types of attire, together with varying modes in the treatment of the hair, sometimes return in slightly different forms years after they had been abandoned for other fashions, so the patterns in the titling of plays are occasionally apt to return unexpectedly. Those which confront us in the Jacobean theatre are, from this point of view, of very particular interest, decidedly evocative.

Their gamut is wide. Thomas Middleton's *A Trick to Catch the Old One* (about 1605) suggestively heads a comedy showing licentious and wasteful wide boys devising schemes for raising cash without working for it; the same author's *A Mad World, My Masters* (about 1606) has a decidedly modern ring, with its implied assumption that all are absurd save the writer and his associates. Occasionally other titles run to length, enigmatically exciting the audience's curiosity, reminiscent of a whole line, in our own days, leading on to *Oh Dad, Poor Dad, Mama's Hung You in the Closet and I'm Feeling So Sad*. Still others are insinuatingly suggestive, like Middleton's *A Chaste Maid in Cheapside* (1611), which might imply that in this district there existed only one such, or his *Viper and Her Brood* (1606), or his later *Women Beware Women* (1621). Some authors, if they did not employ four-letter words, at least made play with five: even Dekker had his *Honest Whore* (1604), a title expanded by John Ford in his *'Tis Pity She's a Whore* about 1630). Some, like William Rowley with his *All's Lost by Lust* (1619), reflect disgust at man's lechery, while others, like John Fletcher with his *Cupid's Revenge* (about 1608), theatrically suggest, almost in modern terms, the dangers arising from sex repression.

Undoubtedly, among these plays there is manifest a vigorous and driving force both in conception and in poetic dialogue, yet few of them exhibit a consistently sustained quality, or, if such quality is present, it exhibits itself rather in the study than on the stage. Middleton's savagely bitter diatribes tend to lose their effect either by their very intensity or by a failure to make palpable to an audience the connections between diverse elements introduced into their structure: thus, in reading *The Changeling* (1622) we can agree that the sub-plot has been designed as an intensifying foil to the powerfully drawn picture of evil presented in the main plot, but in seeing the play spectators are likely to misinterpret the pattern. Comparatively rarely do we encounter here the complex and yet theatrically effective design wrought by Cyril Tourneur in his *Revenger's Tragedy*: in this play the chief emphasis is laid on blanched skulls and chalky bones and dark corridors illuminated by flickering candles; most of Vindice's speeches, among the most memorable to be found in the non-Shakespearean dramas of the age, harmonize with the action by dwelling constantly upon images of lust and death and loathing; but the total impress of the play derives from the author's bold use of two contrasting elements. If the majority of the characters, given names such as Lussurioso, Spurio, Supervacuo, and Sordido, are unrepentingly evil and stupid, they are offset by a Castiza, whose virtue remains untainted by her surroundings, and even by a Gratiana, who, although she is tempted, returns to grace. Still more significant is the second contrasting feature of the play. When Vindice is made to hug himself in ecstacy as he contemplates the skull of his dead mistress –

I'm lost again: you cannot find me yet:
I'm in a throng of happy apprehensions;

when he thinks he "could e'en chide" himself "for doting on her beauty"; when his brother applauds "the quaintness" of his "malice"; and when, at the close, they both gleefully ex-

press to the old Lord Antonio satisfied pride in their cleverness
and ingenuity –

> *Hippolito:*   'Twas all done for the best, my lord.
> *Vindice:*   All for your grace's good. We may be bold to
> speak it now; 'twas somewhat witty carried,
> though we say it. 'Twas we two murdered him.
> *Antonio:*   You two?
> *Vindice:*   None else, i'faith, my lord; nay, 'twas well
> manag'd.
> *Antonio:*   Lay hands upon these villains.
> *Vindice:*   How? on us?
> *Antonio:*   Bear 'em to speedy execution.
> *Vindice:*   Heart, was't not for your good, my lord?
> *Antonio:*   My good?
> Away with 'em! Such an old man as he:
> You that would murder him would murder me.
> *Vindice:*   Is't come about?
> *Hippolito:*   'Sfoot, brother, you begun –

we realize how much the sardonic humour and irony enrich
and give arresting balance to the central theme of the play.

Tourneur's drama is itself a foil, serving in its own way to
suggest what many of his fellows failed to produce. That it is
not a truly great masterpiece may be admitted; that *Volpone*
surpasses it as a work of literature may be agreed; but it does
possess a theatrical potency and a balanced quality of its own.
Certainly it has much more of these than such a man as poor,
puzzled, perplexed Chapman could attain. This translator of
The Iliad and *The Odyssey*, who claimed that Homer's ghost
had actually appeared to him in a vision in order to set a wreath
upon his English descendent's head, strove hard to find a philosophic answer to man's problem and to express this answer in
dramatic terms. At first his hero was Achilles, and Achilles,
conceived as the passionate superman, led him towards intensi-
fication of Marlowe's concept of those rare souls who strive
beyond the scope of ordinary mortals. The central character
in *Bussy D'Ambois* (1604) is thus put before us as a defiant
individualist, a prime triumph of Nature's workmanship who
has no doubt concerning his own excellence,

> A man of spirit beyond the reach of fear
> Who (discontent with his neglected worth)
> Neglects the light, and loves obscure abodes.

Remembering the cult of darkness expressed in *The Shadow of Night*, we can have no doubt that in the presentation of Bussy the author is consciously giving us a projection of what he himself was, or at least of what he dreamed of being, a man "who to himself is law", and therefore who

> no law doth need,
> Offends no law, and is a king indeed.

He realizes – from his own experience – that even such "a complete man", so admirably fashioned by Nature, is doomed by Nature herself to be destroyed, and hence he inclines to see this creative force as ultimately animated by envy : the almost superhuman hero,

> Young, learned, valiant, virtuous and full-mann'd,
> One on whom Nature spent so rich a hand
> That with an ominous eye she wept to see
> So much consum'd her virtuous treasury,

is fated to be destroyed like Tamburlaine and Faustus, and at his death there can remain only an epitaph, characteristically put into the mouth of the enigmatic Friar's ghost –

> Farewell, brave relics of a complete man.
> Look up and see thy spirit made a star;
> Join flames with Hercules, and, when thou sett'st
> Thy radiant forehead in the firmament,
> Make the vast crystal crack with thy receipt.

Bussy D'Ambois, however, has a sequel in *The Revenge of Bussy D'Ambois*, written some six years later, and in the meantime Chapman has moved into a different sphere of thought. Instead of Achilles, his hero has become the wisely stalwart Ulysses, and consequently he invents in that hero's image the figure of Bussy's brother, Clermont, who is described as excelling in virtue his murdered kinsman –

> because, besides his valour,
> He hath the crown of man and all his parts,
> Which learning is; and that so true and virtuous

That it gives power to do as well as say
Whatever fits a most accomplished man,
Which Bussy, for his valour's season, lack'd,
And so was rapt with outrage oftentimes
Beyond decorum.

And thus Chapman, changing his point of view, could move into the camp of the Stoics: Nature's omnipotence, although often incomprehensible, could grimly be accepted, and the superman could become a figure arousing admiration by his adroit outwitting of life's straits and obstacles.

This selection of Chapman's two plays for particular, even if necessarily brief, examination is to be excused because, for all his eccentricity, this author stands centrally in the Jacobean age. We turn back to Tourneur, for example, and note that *The Revenger's Tragedy*, too, has a later counterpart, *The Atheist's Tragedy* (about 1611), and when we further observe that its hero is named Claremont we immediately recognize that there exists an intimate and consciously wrought connection between this character and Chapman's Clermont. And beyond such precise parallels it is evident that many of the dramatists of the time were concerned with the same basic thoughts and puzzlements as afflicted the minds of those two authors. We have, indeed, only to cast our gaze a few years backward in order to sense, in Hamlet's wondering speech about man in his relationship to animal nature and to the hierarchy of the angels, Shakespeare's intense concern with the same essential problem.

Bussy D'Ambois is, in its own way, a fascinating composition, yet, considered as a piece for the theatre, it cannot be deemed successful: given a good actor in the leading rôle, it may sporadically arouse that admiration which obviously Chapman desired to stimulate, but as a whole it fails, and closer examination shows that John Dryden, with his usual perspicacity, accurately summed up its weakness. "When I had taken up what I supposed a fallen star," he wrote,

I found I had been cozened with a jelly: nothing but a cold dull mass, which glittered no longer than it was shooting; a dwarfish thought dressed up in gigantic words, repetition in abundance, looseness of expression and gross hyperboles, the sense of one line expanded prodigiously into ten; and to sum up all, incorrect English, and a hideous mingle of false poetry and true nonsense; or at best, a scantling of wit, which lay gasping for life, and groaning beneath a heap of rubbish.

Harsh words certainly, yet, if the play be considered as a play, not unjustified. We approach closer to success in John Webster's *The Duchess of Malfi* (1614) and *The White Devil* (1612), with their visions of darkness which are fitfully and luridly illuminated by palace candles and torches. These plays do bear revival, although even their appeal must inevitably be limited. In the latter Webster immediately indicated the school to which he belongs by giving chief praise in his preface to the "full and heightened style of Master Chapman" and "the laboured and understanding works of Master Jonson"; as in the dramas of those authors, balance and contrast are lacking. Here we are given a picture, with but little relief, of corrupt and vicious life, almost its only positive quality resting in the vigorous animal vitality of the heroine and the rancorous, perhaps it would be better to say rancid, moralistic materialism of her companion Flamineo; and even although the former play offers us the well-known pitiful portrait of the duchess, its canvas is as dark in colour, depicting a world debased and made ugly by man's evil passions. It must be admitted that Webster has distinction among his companions because of the wider poetic range of his imagination; where so many of the others can achieve nothing memorable save when they are berating the universe or angrily vomiting their disgust, he can at times find thrillingly effective words to express other emotions. Yet these works, although they offer popular material for anthologies, have had but limited stage appeal in later times. Even during their own days we may question whether they made any real impact upon more than a restricted number of spectators: in the printed text of *The White Devil* the author notes the failure of its *première*, attributing this chiefly to the fact that it was acted on a "dull" day "in time of winter", but maybe the lack of applause was due to the inner or spiritual gloom of his scenes.

There are times when young poets of the kind exemplified in these playwrights, while doing their best to offer their public a shocking view of the world, reveal their own inadequacy and defeat their own ends by indulging in what might be described as a perverse or inverted sentimentalism, expressed in various ways and exhibiting many inconsistencies. In such ages we generally discover that while they cry out bitterly

O were I dead, how happy should I be!

or attack the excesses of the rich, they want both to stay alive and to enjoy the licentious wealth against which they fulminate. The cult of the youthful needy hero, so common a character in the lighter plays of the Jacobean period, is one prominent manifestation of such inconsistency. Sometimes the inconsistency is revealed in an ironically comical manner, and then, precisely because we feel that the authors are at least half-smiling at themselves, a certain balance is preserved. One example will serve. About the year 1615 three authors, Middleton, William Rowley, and Philip Massinger, wrote a play called *The Old Law; or A New Way to Please You,* a fantastic piece set in a country where, instead of receiving old-age pensions, men at sixty and women at fifty are summarily disposed of. Although the piece in its entirety has only limited merit, individual scenes, such as that showing a husband bribing a parish clerk to falsify his mate's birth record or that presenting a wife, whose husband is nearing the fatal age, openly receiving suitors for her hand, are both exceedingly funny and startlingly modern in tone. But fantasies like this are rare. Much more typical are the various plays in which several young authors engaged in their private 'War of the Theatres', or in which satire formed the chief interest – for, as Marston expressed it in his *What You Will,*

I cannot tell, 'tis now grown fashion,
What's out of railing's out of fashion –

or in which 'wit' is the main ingredient, as in Middleton and William Rowley's *Wit at Several Weapons* (1609) and John Fletcher's *Wit without Money* (1614), or in which the Jacobean malady, melancholia, is displayed in guises from the humorous to the mad.

It was in this world that the second half of Shakespeare's life was spent; within its years many of his most notable dramas were composed. Although it would be inappropriate to examine any of these works individually in a short impressionistic historical sketch such as this, there is the necessity here of trying to set their author in his Jacobean environment. That he was deeply influenced by that environment is certain: indeed, it may almost be claimed that at times he became so enveloped in it as to lose his masterly grip on the drama. Some of the diatribes in *Timon of Athens*, for example, come perilously close to matching the abandoned, bitter misanthropy in which others attacked man and his society. At the same time, even while observing how the spirit of the age is mirrored in his writings, we must still be careful to note the basic difference between him and his companions – and perhaps we should be even more careful to avoid two pitfalls, that of interpreting his plays as though their author were a Tourneur or a Webster, and that of assuming that they were consciously, intellectually devised expositions of a formal social-philosophical thesis. The stature of *Hamlet*, and indeed its inherent worth to us today, becomes miserably reduced if the Prince of Denmark is treated simply as an angry, confused, and baffled adolescent, or if he becomes merely a psychoanalytic specimen of the Oedipus complex, or if the entire tragedy is explained in terms of 'Renaissance man' struggling to free himself from the trammels of medievalism.

The truth seems to be that, in general, Shakespeare's distinction from his companions, and therefore the chief explanation of his enduring quality, rests in the fact that, while they became personally involved, he remained a kind of Aeolian harp producing music from the air which swirled about him. Several features of the plays he wrote during the early years of the seventeenth century illustrate this clearly. Only two of his dramas come close, in language and invective mood, to the ironic disgust expressed by his fellows. The first of these is *Troilus and Cressida* (about 1601), and it is significant that this peculiar play has every appearance of having been designed, on commission, for performance before a special select audience (probably at one of the Inns of Court), while other evidence suggests that it was never publicly performed during Shakespeare's lifetime. Even so, however, its quality is still different from that of the other plays we have been considering:

the filthy spittings of Thersites, the impotent lechery of Pandarus, and the sexual luxury of Helen and Cressida combine to present a picture of folly, treachery, lust, and false pride, yet even here a vision beyond the limits of the immediate picture is plainly palpable. Only in *Timon of Athens* does the dramatist seem to have lost his footing – and it is significant that this play appears almost certainly to have been abandoned by its author in an uncompleted state: there is every reason to believe that it never was presented before a contemporary audience.

Another observation may here be made. During those years when comedy was turning so often to satirical realism, Shakespeare avoided the form completely. This seemingly was a realm which his genius could not inhabit. Not uninteresting is the fact that the only scene in all his plays wherein he made direct definite reference to contemporary conditions is the passage in *Hamlet* alluding to the success of the child-actors – and, as we have seen, it was within the private theatres used by those players that the satiric play chiefly found its home.

On the other hand, he could not escape being affected by the current developments of the tragic stage, and in this sphere the winds undoubtedly caused the Aeolian harp to produce at times marvellous discordant music. With the exception of the early *Titus Andronicus* (about 1590), the fancifully lyrical *Romeo and Juliet* (about 1595), and the more serious among the chronicle-histories, he had kept himself aloof from this kind of play until the very close of the sixteenth century; thereafter, following the writing of *Julius Caesar* (about 1599), he devoted himself almost exclusively to tragedy for a period of some seven or eight years; and in these dramas, obviously, he revealed many aspects of human evil and brutality. In none of them, however, does the beast in man completely rule the stage: in contradistinction to so many other playwrights of the period who showed themselves incapable of recognizing the existence of goodness or, if they recognized it, of displaying it with any sense of conviction, Shakespeare in his tragedies weighs good and evil on the scales. The discordances are wrought into a symphony through their association with melodic patterns: the world of *King Lear* (about 1605) is dark; in this darkness devilry takes possession of many souls, torment and madness have to be endured; but there is still Cordelia's love, there is still Kent's loyal devotion, there is even the unexpected and characteristic upsurging of honest human feeling displayed – we might almost say symbolically – in the unnamed servant who dares to stand up against Regan and Cornwall and who dies in his attempt to protect Gloucester.

Several other features of these tragedies deserve attention when they are put alongside other tragedies of the time. In all the four 'great' plays we are given, as it were, studies of heroes perplexed – Hamlet perplexed by his environment and conflicting duties, Othello perplexed by Iago's insinuations and his own inner nature, Lear perplexed by the results of his own folly and by the impact of resolutely vicious evil, Macbeth perplexed by diabolic influences both from without and from within. These characters assume a dramatic rôle entirely different from that, say, of Tourneur's Vindice : for him there is no perplexity, rather is there complete assurance, and as a consequence the pattern of evil tends to become shapeless and blurred.

The comparison with Tourneur's drama suggests something else: we become fully conscious of the fact that Shakespeare's poetically conceived vision of evil surpasses in intensity other similar visions because of its 'reality'. Although *The Revenger's Tragedy* has genuine theatrical force and balance, its impact upon the audience becomes blunted by two elements in its structure – the two-dimensional, almost caricature-like, presentation of its characters, and the clearly contrived planning of its action – elements which are to be discerned in numerous plays of this period, making us both conscious of artificiality and suspicious of exaggeration. Compared with the central figures in these works, the persons inhabiting *Lear*'s ancient Britain, *Macbeth*'s savage Scotland, *Hamlet*'s harsh Denmark, and *Othello*'s distant Venice seem to be living human beings; the Witches appear not to be figments of the imagination; Iago is not simply a fabricated monster. And, finally, we cannot escape noticing that Shakespeare, precisely because his vision of evil *is* real, is enabled to keep himself free from the current, and largely artificial, exploitation of youth's disillusionment and the callous viciousness of age. Instead, he gives us a complete circle, with studies of life's misery and torment suffered by heroes extending from a youthful Wittenberg student, through a vigorous middle-aged general and a brave soldier somewhat declined into the vale of years, on to a father four-score and upward.

When we take all these features together under consideration, we begin to realize why, on the stage, Shakespeare's plays offer us a satisfaction absent in contemplation of the others. *Volpone* leaves us with a picture of men turned into beasts – nothing more; sardonic disgust gives *The Revenger's Tragedy* its prevailing flavour; the mood predominant in Webster's dramas is despair at contemplating human depravity. Unless when they are twisted out of shape, these tragedies of Shakespeare's, despite their horrors, do not send us out of the theatre either depressed or cynically morose.

In this connection one of Shakespeare's latest dramas, although perhaps not to be counted among his greatest achievements, has particular interest. When he was a young man he had penned a dream of an enchanted midsummer eve, a dream which at moments fleetingly took on the confused pattern of a nightmare; now, at the close of his career, he turned to compose *A Winter's Tale* (1610). In this play of a dark December death rudely enters in, Antigonus is savaged by a bear on a lonely coast, and the wretched little prince Mamillius pines away in grief. The drama, then, cannot be taken merely as a comedy: yet the extraordinary thing is that all the characters in it are essentially good – and in using that word 'good' we cannot escape feeling ourselves in the presence, not of any cloistered virtue, but of virtue dynamic in quality. It is true that one man, Leontes, is responsible for the death of his son and, incidentally at least, for the loyal Antigonus' demise, and the responsibility is shown to be his alone. In three earlier plays Shakespeare had similarly dealt with the excesses of jealousy, causing those passions to be kindled and enflamed by an outside agency evil in intent. Here in *A Winter's Tale* there exists no Don John, no Iago, no Iachimo : daringly, the poet has made the poisonous thoughts well up from within the husband's own being and he has supremely demonstrated his dramatic skill by making it easy for us to move so understandingly and sympathetically from the King's ugly ravings in the first act to his contrition in the last. This contrition is not simply a convenient dramatic trick; apart from the momentary jealous passion which grips

F

him, Leontes is shown inherently dignified, upright, and honest. As for the rest, Polixenes and his son, Camillo, Antigonus and Cleomenes, Hermione and Perdita, Paulina – their minds and affections are untainted by any corruption; even the a-moral Autolycus is a good-hearted rogue, and grey-bearded Time is kindly compassionate.

Only a few short seasons separated this play from Jonson's *Volpone*. In producing the latter play at Minneapolis in 1964 Sir Tyrone Guthrie observed that it includes "no virtuous characters" – a generalization which may be thought to be a trifle wide, since Jonson did bring in his innocent Celia and Bonario, and yet no doubt the modern director was right in so treating this pair as to suggest that their shallow simplicity, in the midst of all the corruption around them, is itself a vice. Comparing the two dramas by Shakespeare and Jonson, we might be tempted to proceed further and dismiss the former as sentimental: but, if we do, we ought to remember that the picture presented in *Volpone* is equally sentimental in its own way. Indeed, looking closely, we realize that the scope of the first is infinitely wider and its perceptions more keen than those in the other. When Leontes cries out in agony –

> Affection! thy intention stabs the centre.
> Thou dost make possible things not so held,
> Communicat'st with dreams – how can this be? –
> With what's unreal thou coactive art,
> And fellow'st nothing –

or –

> There may be in the cup
> A spider steep'd, and one may drink, depart,
> And yet partake no venom, for his knowledge
> Is not infected; but if one present
> Th' abhorr'd ingredient to his eye, make known
> How he hath drunk, he cracks his gorge, his sides,
> With violent hefts. I have drunk, and seen the spider –

we are aware that paradoxically we are being confronted by a more real and vividly imagined devilish potency than appears in any of the artificial figments created by the Jacobean theatre of disgust.

6

Courtly
Elegance

In 1964 a dramatic critic declared that our latest, contemporary dramatic 'revolution' has marked the first revival of British playwriting for 350 years. Three hundred and fifty years from 1964 brings us back to 1614, just about the time when *King Henry VIII*, probably Shakespeare's final dramatic effort, was produced and when the Jacobean experiments in satirical realism and in bizarre artificiality were showing signs of losing their force.

This declaration is clearly based on three implicit assumptions – (*1*) that the present wave of new dramatists has been so mighty as to bring its crest close to the height of Shakespeare's achievement, (*2*) that the wave has surged suddenly upward with a power entirely unexpected from an unrippled watery waste, and (*3*) that from about 1614 to about 1956 the English drama is without interest, uninspired and uninspiring, produc-

real masters. In our excitement over the recent 'revolu-
erhaps a little exaggeration may be legitimate, yet these
........implied assumptions require to be closely examined before they can be accepted: and, in particular, it is essential
that we should scrutinize carefully the theatre's activities during those long centuries from the beginning of the seventeenth
century on to the middle of the twentieth.

There can, of course, be not the slightest doubt that after the
close of Shakespeare's career a slow but clearly marked decline
in theatrical vigour becomes manifest. For the most part, plays
of the kind associated with the names of Marston, Tourneur,
and Webster gradually disappeared: Middleton's dark tragicomedy *The Witch* may have come forward during the middle
years of James' reign and certainly his *Changeling* and *Women
Beware Women* seem to belong to the early twenties, yet even
this author in *A Fair Quarrel*, written about 1616, showed an
alteration in style, and much of his time was devoted to the
penning of masques and 'entertainments'. Obviously a new
mood was at work in the playhouses.

In order to appreciate the conditions which led to the establishment of this new mood it is necessary to remember that when
the Commonwealth regime was established in 1642 one of
its first acts was summarily to shut up the theatres, and since
Oliver Cromwell came to power as leader of a movement which
had been steadily building up its strength during the decades
immediately preceding we need feel no surprise in finding ourselves advancing into a world different from the Elizabethan
and early Jacobean and in encountering an audience socially
and spiritually far distant from our own. Present-day Puritans
have embraced the theatre, but in that earlier period the Puritans, beginning to strengthen their grip upon the populace,
declared the playhouse to be the home of the devil. William
Prynne's bulky and compendious *Histriomastix* in 1633 provided them with an encyclopedic work of reference concerning
the stage's vices and in every respect reflected their uncompro-
mising hostility to players and playwrights. In an age when
indexes to books were very rare this volume was provided with
a 'table' which boldly draws attention to its 'chiefest passages',
and these chiefest passages mince no words: "Men's wearing
of women's, and women's putting on of men's apparel", we are

told, is an "Abomination to the Lord"; acting, whether "for gain or pleasure", is "infamous, unlawful, and that as well in Princes, Nobles, Gentlemen, Scholars, Divines as common Actors"; players are "most desperate wicked wretches", "professed agents and instruments of the Devil", while "Playhaunters" are "the worst and lewdest persons, for the most part"; theatres are "dens of lewdness and filthiness, schools of bawdry and uncleanliness, stews of shame and immodesty, shops of Satan, the plagues of men's souls", in fact "a Babylonish brothel", "always full of devils, who claim them as their own". True, a reading of contemporary ballads and other popular literature suggests that the final establishment of the Commonwealth was effected not so much by a general puritanization and upsurging of the ordinary folk as by the deployment of highly trained and ideologically indoctrinated storm-troopers: nevertheless, the country was rapidly being split into two sections, so that increasingly the playhouses became the recognized haunts of the 'Cavaliers' and their associates.

For these men and their ladies the theatre meant primarily entertainment, and consequently the products of the new wave of dramatists who had flourished during the century's first decade lost their clientele. In all probability, however, their plays would in any case have ceased to appeal; they had succeeded in arresting attention because of their novelty in style, and on repetition novelty is apt to become boring if not nauseous. These writers had based their effects largely on shock-treatment, on exploitation of human corruption, on blackness lit by lurid flashes of artificial illumination. In doing so they were certainly responsible for a dramatic revolution, or, as Shakespeare styled it, an 'innovation'. But the trouble with shock-treatment is that, with the passage of years, the shocks must be so increased as eventually to result in killing all interest; the trouble with the constant display of corruption is, as has been suggested, that in the end it is inclined to veer towards the sentimental; and, while blackness and lurid flashes of illumination may at first succeed in riveting the attention of the public, after a short time the spectators tend to become afflicted with eye-strain. It seems, therefore, most probable that the vogue, quite apart from possible alterations in the quality of the audience, was of a kind destined to run only a brief course.

In any event, the new generation of playgoers began to call for diversity in the theatre, for the exhibition of adroit and supple technical skill, for the presentation upon the stage of such a smoothness and elegance as might correspond with the elegance and ease of their own social surroundings; and in making these demands they gradually helped to shape the dramatic forms of the future. Even though the 'well-made' play was not yet born, its basic features were being formed in embryo.

Among the limited number of serious dramas belonging to this later style which have been selected for revival during recent years, present-day audiences have had the chance of seeing *The Maid's Tragedy* (about 1609), one of the earliest collaborative efforts of Francis Beaumont and John Fletcher, as well as two works by John Ford, *'Tis Pity She's a Whore* (about 1632) and *The Broken Heart* (about 1630) – and, since these are characteristic of the new moods, with them we may begin.

Actually, *The Maid's Tragedy* comes before the year 1614, and it is entirely possible that its *première* occurred in the same year as that of *The Atheist's Tragedy*. No two plays, however, could be more unlike each other: the one belongs to the early Jacobean movement, the other points unmistakably towards something quite different. Tourneur, in penning his drama of the atheist, unquestionably had his mind set on expressing an idea: the moral content of his work was of more consequence to him than its artistic form. Equally clearly, the two young men who joined in writing their play about an unfortunate maid, were intent upon fashioning a play in which a skilfully planned story was of chief importance.

These young men belonged to the same social milieu as that which was beginning to embrace the playhouse, and in this they stood distinct from the run of professional dramatists preceding them. Almost all of the latter had been humbly born; even Shakespeare, whose mother had certain pretensions to minor 'gentle' birth, came from a provincial bourgeois environment. Beaumont and Fletcher, on the other hand, were gentlemen born, one the son of a judge, the other of a bishop; and, intimately acquainted with what the new public wanted, they wrought their tragedy with the objective of attracting the spectators' interest through the exercise of elegance and adroit showmanship.

In saying this, however, perhaps we should also observe that in a sense they had been anticipated by the sensitively perceptive Shakespeare. Presumably not all those who frequented the theatre during the first decade of the seventeenth century delighted in nothing save the plays of Marston, Tourneur, and their companions; undoubtedly among the assembled body of spectators were men and women not markedly dissimilar in their tastes from those who later took the playhouses into their keeping, and perhaps Shakespeare was thinking largely of them when in 1603 or 1604 he wrote his *Othello*. *Othello* obviously assumes a form different from that of his other tragedies: although distanced in Venice, its atmosphere is almost domestic, and its characters are somewhat different from those presented in *Macbeth* and *King Lear*; its structure is taut and its story told in straightforward manner; and, most important of all, this story is one of strange love and passionate jealousy. Although racialism had not become a strong force at that period, audiences would certainly have been titillated by the sight of an aristocratic girl wedded to a swarthy Moor and by witnessing a scene of grim vengeance in a bedroom. When we observe how frequently *Othello* was imitated during the later 'Cavalier' age we need not hesitate to see in it the pattern which inspired *The Maid's Tragedy* and its successors both in content and in form.

In *The Maid's Tragedy* we find ourselves, as the play begins, in the midst of colourful preparations for a royally sponsored wedding. A King has seen fit to show his favour to a loyal young courtier by bidding him marry a beautiful lady of the Court; and the bridegroom, who had long looked upon her as a star, is in an ecstacy of delight and anticipation. The wedding feast, with its rich accompaniment of a masque, draws to its close, and the couple are ceremoniously led to their bridal chamber. Arrived there, the young bride, in blunt terms, informs her husband that she is, in fact, the King's mistress, that the marriage has been arranged solely for the royal convenience. In rage he lashes out at her with searing words, words that so penetrate her callousness that she is led not only to see the horror of her actions but to develop a strange passion for her husband of convenience. Although the plot is complicated by the presence of an Aspatia, who had previously been affianced to the hero, and of the bride's brothers Melantius and Diphilus, in essence all the action leads up to the two scenes when the wife murders the King as he lies in bed and then in dismay hears her husband recoil in horror when he learns of her crime of regicide.

This story, told smoothly and expertly both in the conduct of its action and in the flow of its vivid and direct although not very profound verse, possesses a quality entirely at variance with that which is apparent in so many of the earlier Jacobean dramas. From an account of its main theme we might well have thought that the authors would have drawn a bitter picture of a corrupt and dark palace, but, in fact, although the King acts arbitrarily and thoughtlessly, the Court is not corrupt; neither the imagery nor the general atmosphere gives even faint hints of any general disgust. The characters are not delineated as symbols of bestial vices; they are depicted not as satirically conceived monsters, but as individuals such as the politer part of the audience might have known and respected. The contrived love plot thus is closely attached to a known reality – but every means has been employed to give it such a novel appearance as to excite and titillate the audience's emotions, and in particular the authors have made use of a new kind of surprise technique. While this surprise technique was no doubt suggested by the shock technique employed by their immediate predecessors, it has a wholly different objective. The earlier shock device had been introduced with the aim of startling spectators into terror and disgust; the surprises cultivated by Beaumont and Fletcher, both in this play and in many later works, were designed merely to keep the spectators' attention wakeful and alert: they were, indeed, a kind of practical demonstration of wit.

Of course, every playgoer who went to see a drama called *The Maid's Tragedy* knew that the play's action would be calamitous: there was no cheating on the authors' part here. Yet the general arrangement of the plot is different from that of almost all preceding tragedies: these had started with premonitions of disaster to come, whereas here the opening scenes with the preparations for the wedding and the distraction of the inserted masque are invested with no darker a suggestion than that the hero, in this marriage, has abandoned a girl with whom he previously had been in love – no ghost as in *Hamlet*, no witches as in *Macbeth*, no wild rage as in *Lear*.

It need hardly be said that this surprise technique, especially when it was more blatantly employed, of necessity inclined towards a lowering of tragic tension. In tragedy we do not want any exhibitions of dramatic cleverness; we are deeply moved only when we are confronted by an action which seems to move forward with terrifying inevitability. This being so, we can understand that, although Beaumont and Fletcher, together with other dramatists, applied themselves to dramas of this kind, they found a new type of play better suited to their purposes, a type in which the surprise was made to work in reverse. *A King and No King*, first acted about the same time as *The Maid's Tragedy*, offers an excellent example. This also is a piquant story-drama, skilfully narrated and theatrically arresting. During the first four acts we find ourselves immersed in a tale of illicit emotions which seemingly can end only in disaster. A young king, struggle inwardly as he may, becomes obsessed by an incestuous passion for his sister : it would appear as though a dismal tragic close to the drama is inevitable – when suddenly, to his complete surprise and largely to ours, the discovery is made that in fact his birth is not royal and that his supposed sister is his queen. In this piece the authors' adroitness has been magnificently displayed, and we may admit that the surprise trick in reverse, leading to what they themselves called 'unexpected comedy' and to what might also be described as thwarted tragedy, can produce effective theatrical results: yet the clever, elegant ease with which the action is made to turn from the threatening rumble of tragic drums to the ringing of royal marriage bells – the way in which the entire play has been planned to lead up to the surprise – emphasizes the rather facile and shallow treatment of both its theme and characters. The well-made drama, especially the well-made drama intent upon exploiting sexual relations, is here being offered to us in completer form.

The surprise technique, as might have been expected, was found to be of almost infinite variation, and perhaps it may be well to take one other example in order both to suggest its scope and to stress its particular application. About 1610 appeared *Philaster* in which the title-rôle hero is shown in love with, and beloved by, the princess Arethusa. One day, walking in the country, he encounters a boy Bellario, makes him his page, sends him with messages to the princess, and eventually hands him over into her service. Evil tongues begin to wag; Arethusa is accused of being unchaste with the lad; Philaster, hearing these whispers, reviles his mistress and comes close to killing Bellario. Only towards the close of the play, when the page deliberately incites the hero to a fight and is slain, do we discover that in reality the youth was a girl who, pining hopelessly for Philaster's love, had assumed male attire in order to be near him.

Comparison of this plot with the plots of two Shakespearian plays helps to show what Beaumont and Fletcher were doing. First, *Twelfth Night*. The central situation in *Philaster* is akin to Viola's dressing as a youth, serving Orsino, and unwillingly going on love missions to Olivia. But here there is no surprise: Shakespeare wants the audience to be in the know from the very start. Although a modern revival of *Philaster*, with an actress in the pathetic lead, would set the audience guessing, Jacobean spectators unfamiliar with the play, seeing a boy-actor as a boy and without any direction from the dramatists, would be unlikely to penetrate the secret. Where Shakespeare conjures his comedy out of his auditors' omniscience, therefore, the other two playwrights choose to rely on concealment and shock. Second, *A Winter's Tale*. Here, certainly, the fact that Hermione has been preserved for many years is carefully kept dark, but whereas in *Philaster* the page's secret inadvertently causes all the complexities of the plot, Hermione's preservation does not affect the plot in any way save that she doubly confirms the atmosphere of calm and reconciliation which has been established by other means.

Before we smile at Beaumont and Fletcher's theatricalism, however, maybe it is worth while noting that just such surprise devices are widely spread over our modern theatre, both the popular and the *élite*. Could we not cite dozens of plays in which an apparently idiotic youth turns out to be an astute detective or a seemingly feckless old lady is revealed as a clever spy? And among *avant-garde* plays do we not frequently encounter characters established as one thing and later shown to be another? The trick, or the device, is not by any means confined to the seventeenth century.

In the hands of Beaumont and Fletcher the theatricalism inherent in the employment of the surprise technique tends to be associated with an accompanying theatricalism in the delineation of the characters and in the subject-matter of the dramas. Within this world of illicit, abnormal, or sentimentally pathetic situations, where the persons strangely meander among their conflicting passions, we sense a tendency towards simplification of the emotions until finally we are left with a world in which only two main passions – love and honour – are pitted against each other. "Oh!" cries a character in one of these plays,

> Oh! furious desire, how like a whirlwind
> Thou hurriest me beyond mine honour's point!

And this sentiment was fated to dominate the area of tragedy and thwarted tragedy for generations.

The two other recently revived tragedies from this period, *'Tis Pity She's a Whore* and *The Broken Heart*, belong to the early years of King Charles' reign, the works of a poet who attempted to steer the drama of love into another channel. He likewise had his theatricalities, but in essence he sought to frame his stage actions out of a study of abnormal psychology. That he was the master of a muted, sometimes pathetic, individual poetic style is certain; equally certain is the fact that his characters are invested with an inner life rarely or never to be found in the writings of Beaumont and Fletcher; but hardly more than theirs do his plays give us an impression of real power. We are enveloped here in an atmosphere which is summed up in the title of another of his works – this truly is a universe of *Lovers' Melancholy* (1628).

What was lacking in these love tragedies may be vaguely discerned if we turn to the writings of still another dramatist, one whom many Victorians regarded as second only to Shakespeare but who now tends to be ignored. Philip Massinger was a serious man and dignified, one who displayed, as in *The Great Duke of Florence* (1627), the best in Cavalier ideals, yet unfortunately he was not gifted with Ford's poetic abilities: rhetoric was his most effective medium, and rhetoric in the theatre, unless it is rendered stylistically thrilling, is apt to become boring. Among his writings there are many in which the cultivation of the love theme is dominant, and it may be confessed that perhaps he, even more than Beaumont and Fletcher, fashioned the mould from which were cast those numerous, monotonously repetitive 'Love and Honour' dramas in the years to come. Only too often his heroes and his heroines are engaged in arguing with themselves or with others on a plane of simplified emotions, almost as though they were holding up scales with the one counterbalancing the other: thus, for example, does Cleora, in *The Bondman*, weigh up her love and duty to two suitors: she feels compelled to think of

Marullo's dangers – though I save his life,
His love is unrewarded – I confess
Both have deserved me; yet, of force, must be
Unjust to one : such is my destiny.

Had all Massinger's plays been of this kind he would hardly have warranted attention here : neither Ford's subtlety nor Fletcher's attractive vigour is present in his works. What, however, is of real interest is his attempt at times to search out other and broader themes – the conflicts of Paganism and Christianity in *The Virgin Martyr* (1620), of faith and expediency in *The Renegado* (1624), of artistic integrity and loyalty in *The Roman Actor* (1626). Even although we may be compelled to admit that all of these plays lack true fire, in reading them we realize how much the tragic stage of that period had lost in its preoccupation with sexual, and often with abnormally sexual, passions.

This sense of loss is still further increased if we turn to consider two exceptional dramas of the early thirties. By that time the chronicle-history play had long since been abandoned by the dramatists, but suddenly in 1631 Massinger applied himself to the penning of a drama about that King Sebastian of Portugal who, presumably slain in battle with the Spaniards, was reputed by legend to have lived on miserably for a number of years, treated as a pretender by former friends and by enemies alike : when the censor made objections to the piece the author, calling it *Believe as You List*, changed the scene to the period of the Roman Empire and altered his hero into

Antiochus the Great. About the same time Ford rather un-
accountably elected to move out of his realm of love in order
to write his *Perkin Warbeck*, dealing with the impostor who,
supported by the King of France, the Emperor Maximilian I,
and, especially, by King James IV of Scotland, claimed to be
England's rightful monarch. Both are effective plays, offering
interesting character studies, the one of a true king caught in a
web of chicanery and political circumstances, the other of a
man who, unquestionably a pretender, exhibits greater royalty
of spirit than those rightfully born to their thrones. No doubt
neither Massinger's work nor Ford's can be regarded as an
outstanding masterpiece, yet both authors were attempting
something fresh: these plays have a modern flavour, and by
indirection at least they once more demonstrate how im-
poverished the mid-seventeenth-century stage was becoming
through its usual exploitation of the amorous passions.

This reflection receives even profounder emphasis when we
turn from Massinger's serious dramas to his darkly comic *A
New Way to Pay Old Debts* (1621), which gave to its central
character, Sir Giles Overreach, his truly amazing theatrical
career. When this play is read, or when it is seen on the stage,
we realize that here was the realm which Massinger ought
chiefly to have inhabited – and further, we recognize that the
cavalier playhouse as a whole, although it failed to produce
any great tragedies, had in it an inspiring comic force. *A New
Way to Pay Old Debts* fully justifies its long-enduring popularity: Overreach, invested with a power which makes him
even more impressive than Jonson's Volpone, has given opportunities to a long series of actors (including Edmund Kean)
culminating in Sir Donald Wolfit; its social milieu has been
alertly observed and skilfully presented; unlike so many earlier
similarly planned dramas, it is well balanced, the anger and the
intrigues of the young hero justified by Overreach's potentially
insane rapacity. This truly was Massinger's greatest achievement, but it does not remain entirely alone. The same balance
and the same incisiveness are present, too, in his *City Madam*
(1632), where the comic delineation of Lady Frugal's social
pretensions and extravagant ostentation finds apt contrast in
her husband's modest demeanour and in the dichotomous behaviour of his brother Luke.

These are comedies which, although they deal with an environment long since vanished, are given a universal quality; and at their side stand others, by various authors, conceived in two entirely different modes. Somewhat peculiarly, the play which nowadays most often comes to mind when the names of Beaumont and Fletcher are mentioned – *The Knight of the Burning Pestle* – does not belong to either of these: it is, in fact, a kind of sport, almost if not wholly unique within its own period, conceived in a form so alien to the spirit of the early seventeenth-century stage that its performance about 1607 was a complete failure. Much more characteristic is *The Chances* (about 1617), selected for revival by the Chichester Festival Theatre, a lively and rollicking piece typical of that type of intrigue comedy, influenced directly or indirectly by the Spanish dramatists, which Fletcher and some of his companions knew how to invest with lively and witty gusto. And closely connected with this comedy of intrigue comes the gradual development of a spritely comedy of manners wherein a new kind of lover and his lass – a licentious but likeable young gallant and a mistress merry as he – take centre stage. Towards this form of comedy the Fletcherian *Wild Goose Chase* (1621) leads the way; it is enriched by Richard Brome's dramatic essays in the depiction of modish social behaviour; and finally it begins to assume formal shape in James Shirley's *The Witty Fair One* (1628), *The Lady of Pleasure* (1635), and *Hyde Park* (1632), plays in which the artificial conventions of contemporary society are set against the ordinary natural human passions lying under their veneer.

Audiences of those days evidently found Shirley's style exactly what they wanted – "sober", "discreet", and "sweet-tempered" – and perhaps because of its sobriety and discretion this author's plays never quite succeeded in reaching their ultimate goal; nevertheless, in them lay the spring from which, ripplingly and with irridescent sparkle, flowed the comedies of manners that enriched the stage during the less sober and less inhibited aristocratic age to come.

What then is to be our general judgment concerning the theatrical worth of this period? If we are prepared fully to admit the virtues of comic entertainment its achievements seem not unworthy of attention and even praise; at the same time, maybe its greatest value for us rests less in what it actually accomplished than in what it aimed to do. Here the pattern of the well-made play was being drawn, and, even although the well-made play lies currently under a dark cloud of condemnation, the devices which it employed are still potent in our midst. We may sneer at the surprise tricks so freely exploited in divers plays of this period, yet the surprise trick is a recognized feature in the most modern of dramas; and even if we recognize that many of today's playwrights strive to cultivate new styles of dramatic structure, there is little difficulty in discerning their indebtedness to the past. The old expansive sweep of the Elizabethan theatre suited the needs of a different age, and the vitality still inherent in those cavalier days becomes evident when we consider the way in which the stage at that time was being shaped into fresh forms.

7

*In Good
King Charles'
Golden Days*

THE theatrical Holy Writ currently followed in advanced
circles is no freer from diverse exegesis than is the Biblical. One
body of opinion, as we have seen, would make the English
stage's waste land begin immediately after Shakespeare gave
up writing: a second body of opinion, conscious of what had
been achieved during the latter half of King James' reign and
during the reign of King Charles I, is inclined to take as a dividing-line the closing of the playhouses by Puritan ordinance in
1642; and still a third, realizing the vigour of the later
seventeenth-century theatre, decides that the waste land assumed its desert contours after the passing of that Licensing
Act in 1737 when the Lord Chamberlain's censorship was form-
ally established. Obviously, as we have seen, the period between
about 1614 and 1642 is by no means devoid of interest and
worth; now we must turn to consider what happened when
once more the playhouses opened their doors in 1660.

The Commonwealth had been endured for some eighteen years, and when Charles II returned from his exile most people heaved a sigh of relief: they had suffered quite enough of restraint. Certainly, once the merry monarch had set up his occasionally disreputable Court in Whitehall, many of them looked askance at their King's unconcealed amatory adventures, but maybe even those who looked with disapproval at his way of life allowed their moral condemnation to be tempered secretly by thoughts of the severities and restrictions which had ruled their lives during Oliver Cromwell's days. At first we might have deemed that, after the chastening effected by the Commonwealth, a sober ruler such as Charles I would have been more likely to succeed than the irrepressible Charles II; but we should have been wrong. The King whom Parliament executed in 1649 had assuredly been, like the dramatist Shirley, praiseworthily sober, but his personality was cold; Charles II frequently was most unsober both in drink and in dalliance, but in him there was an appealing warmth and generosity which gave charm to his black-avised countenance – and generous warmth was precisely that of which the English folk had been starved under Puritan control.

The ordinary men and women of the time, however, had for so long been alien to the theatre that, while they accepted and welcomed various other freedoms, they contentedly permitted their new monarch and his Whitehall companions to assume full command of the playhouse. Two relatively small playhouses were thus sufficient to accommodate the restricted audiences of gallants and their ladies throughout a period of twenty years from just after the Restoration in 1660 on to 1682, and for a decade and a half after the latter date the playgoing public became so small that one theatre alone was amply sufficient to cater for their needs. These houses of entertainment, then, may be regarded as having been appendages of the Court, and the conventions associated with them were designed to make them serve more or less as clubs for Charles' bevy of boon companions.

From the midst of such a theatrical world it might well have been thought that nothing could emanate likely to yield present-day appeal; yet out of this apparently unpromising environment arose numbers of plays which still have power to delight and inspire.

The realm of tragedy has, of course, practically nothing to offer us of any value. All the efforts of John Dryden and his fellows in the penning of rimed, rhetorical 'Love and Honour' dramas are now merely historical curiosities, and even when the riming style was abandoned the spirit remained largely the same. We may admit that *All for Love*(1677) is well and expertly planned, and yet still find it lacking in power and insight. Thomas Otway's *Venice Preserv'd* (1682) may bear revival and, in reading at least, his *Orphan* (1680) yields a mild sort of pathetic appeal; but both these plays owe such quality as they possess to the fact that their author instinctively or deliberately sought inspiration in earlier styles of dramatic writing; their most affecting scenes are watered-down versions of what he found in *The Maid's Tragedy* and kindred works. For the rest, there is virtually nothing. Even William Congreve's *The Mourning Bride* (1697), the creation of a major author, is remembered now only – and quite rightly – for its opening line, "Music has charms to soothe a savage breast".

When, on the other hand, we turn to comedy, we are transported into a world entirely different. This same author, Congreve, who concocted such a dismally dull tragedy, was the author of one of the English theatre's most exquisite masterpieces, *The Way of the World* (1700).

The way of the world presented in this and its companion comedies of manners was the way of careless, often riotous, libidinous young gallants. There is no sobriety here; "sweet-tempered" and "discreet" are about the last epithets we should think of applying to them. The girls are racy, the men rapacious, and continually they move in a merry dance, chasing each other, laughingly eluding each other, the girls for the most part tantalizingly flirtatious, intent upon marriage, the gallants anxious to retain their freedom yet risking capture at the close of the chase. And around the gay couples are others – the gentlemen who overstep the bounds of society's codes and thus become ridiculous, the middle-aged ladies who simper and longingly seek, the natural oddities, and the eccentrics.

The one thing which, above all others, distinguishes this world is wit, and the perfection of that wit could not have been

achieved at any earlier period. Wit's expression depends upon
the creation of a supple, easy, epigrammatic, and delicate con-
versational prose style; and it was in this age that the speech
of society threw off its rhetorical shackles, savouring with delight the polish and sparkle of sentences exquisitely poised. In
the development of human cultures poetry usually tends to
attain precise form long before prose is similarly fashioned:
Homer lived ages before Plato, Chaucer before Dryden and
Swift – and it was in the period spanned by these last two men
that English prose, of a kind fitted for easy familiar repartee,
came into its own.

The development of the new comedy, although anticipated
by Dryden and others, first reached assurance in witty Sir
George Etherege's *She Wou'd if She Cou'd* eight years after
the playhouses had been reopened, was caught up by William
Wycherley a few seasons later in *The Gentleman Dancing
Master* and *The Country Wife*, was tossed back to Etherege in
The Man of Mode, produced in 1676, and then, after the lapse
of more than a couple of decades, was gradually brought to final
perfection by Congreve in *The Old Bachelor* (1693), *The
Double Dealer* (1693), *Love for Love* (1695), and *The Way
of the World*.

All these plays are known to us in many revivals. No doubt
their tone is quite reprehensible, and those of us who know our
social history may deplore their complete indifference to the
grime and squalor, the poverty and degradation which lay beyond the privileged circle of the gallants who preened themselves in St James' Park, in the fashionable boudoirs, and in
the drawing-rooms. Yet they have the grace of laughter and
delight. No doubt their heyday in the modern playhouse came
during the thirties, forties, and early fifties of the present
century, but even now, when sterner things appear on the
boards, they can still command attention. Perhaps it is good
for even the most serious and socially dedicated theatre-men to
dwell at least for a brief space within their orbit, and assuredly
some recent productions have given welcome sparkle to theatres
inclined towards gloom and towards humour which is black
and sick. And their worth rests within their own beings. It
would, of course, be very easy to present them on the stage as
Molière's plays have recently seen production in France, with

vignettes introduced between the acts showing the beggars and the sots and the miserable rags of poverty that had their existence beyond the limits of the lively merriment; but that would obscure their real value for us. Not for nothing was dissolute King Charles fondly named "Good"; not for nothing does the historical memory retain a warm affection for morally deplorable, kind-hearted, and generous Nell Gwyn, the actress who was, in effect, the true model and the original creator of the witty heroine whose apotheosis flounces impertinently before us in the person of Millamant.

Can we then say that an age which gave birth to this series of delightful comedies was lacking in dramatic vitality or that its worth to us is negligible? If we are prepared to do so our judgment must depend solely on one consideration – that the theatre of this period produced nothing of serious social content and that comedies which exist primarily for their merriment are to be despised. No doubt such an attitude can be logically adopted by those for whom the stage has value only in so far as it becomes a political instrument; but if we look upon the theatre as an art of wide potentialities and if we see its social value as resting in more than its political message, then we must admit that the Restoration comedies of manners cannot be ignored and despised. Naturally, it is to be deplored that this age failed so completely in its more serious efforts, yet such failure should not lead to disesteem of its masterpieces in comedy; nor need we, in our own democratic days, reject what those young, brilliant, and witty young aristocrats had to offer. They too had their vision of human nature, a vision which frequently went beyond the limits of their own immediate environment: that vision, and the gaiety which accompanied it, retains its original theatrical worth and appeal even in days when the modes and manners of Charles' Court have completely vanished.

8

A Century of
the Genteel and
the Sentimental

SHAKESPEARE'S *Hamlet* must have been put upon the stage about the year 1601: almost exactly a hundred theatrical seasons later Congreve's *The Way of the World* had its *première*. During the entire course of this century dramatic vitality, although at times waxing and waning, preserved its force, and consequently there appears to be no real justification for fixing the frontier of the waste land either immediately after Shakespeare's retirement or after the closing of the theatres in 1642. A comparison of the seventeenth century with that which followed, however, reveals a different perspective view. Even if we refuse to regard it as completely barren, even if, as we must, we give praise to some of its scattered accomplishments, we are compelled to look upon it as an age when theatres were creatively active but when dramatic masterpieces were excessively rare.

Clearly, the first question which we must put to ourselves is, Why? And at the very start it is necessary to consider the third body of current opinion which has already been referred to: this declares that the cause of dramatic decline is to be found in the establishment of the Lord Chamberlain's control, that the censorship drove many distinguished authors to abandon the stage in disgust and to seek scope for the expression of their 'visions' within the field of the novel. Since such assertions have been frequently repeated during the past ten years and since they have been widely accepted, in an uncritical manner, by those interested in the theatre, clearly they demand careful examination. What can be said at once is that the assertions themselves have not the slightest foundation in fact and that they are in themselves essentially sentimental. It is true that the Licensing Act of 1737 put an immediate stop to Henry Fielding's theatrical activities. For some years previously he had been amusing himself with a company of comedians performing in a minor playhouse, and for them he had penned a number of politically satirical pieces, the very skits indeed which stimulated parliamentary action. The Act was passed; his minor playhouse was closed; and he himself turned to the writing of *Tom Jones*. In considering these events, however, we have to bear several things in mind: while it is possible that complete stage freedom might have permitted the development of new dramatic forms, this can be no more than a kind of wishful thinking: Fielding's own burlesque skits were not major works of art and whatever 'vision' they may have had was related in no way to the concept which inspired his great "comic epos in prose": there can be no justification for the assumption that, suddenly prevented from expressing his ideas freely on the stage, he turned to give them expression in his novels. And, if this is true of Fielding, it is equally true of other later novelists. If Sir Walter Scott had possessed dramatic ability not a single scene in any of the *Waverley* series could have met with the censor's disapprobation: indeed, scores of dramatic versions of his novels proved highly popular fare in the playhouses. None of these were written by Scott himself, precisely because, as his few independent dramatic essays indicate, his genius required the wide sweep offered to him in narrative fiction. So, too, with Dickens. Although eagerly interested in the theatre, his original plays clearly indicate that he lacked dramatic power: for him also the expansive scope of the novel was essential; and the numerous stage versions of his prose narratives were made by other and lesser men. With such facts the censorship had absolutely nothing to do. In contemplating the waste land, therefore, it is necessary to seek elsewhere for the conditions likely to explain its arid expanse.

Reference to the Licensing Act has carried us well towards the middle of the eighteenth century and consideration of recent assertions about its force has brought us still further into the Victorian era. Now we must turn back to look at what was happening in the playhouses from the time when *The Way of the World* first made its appearance.

Strangely, this final masterpiece of Congreve's arrived just when a mighty change in theatrical affairs was becoming active, and for this change a puritan, and not a censor, was responsible. Old puritans never die; or at least they continually recreate themselves in diverse forms by spiritual reproduction. When the seventeenth century was drawing to its close William Prynne, author in 1633 of that indigestible anti-theatrical diatribe *Histriomastix*, had been deceased for some thirty years, but in 1698 he was reincarnated in the person of Jeremy Collier, a sour clergyman whose shocked account of the immorality and profaneness of the contemporary stage fluttered dramatists and audiences alike. The former either feebly sought to refute his accusations or supinely put on the cap of penitence; the latter, or at least some of them, proceeded to form societies for the improvement of manners, especially of manners on the stage.

Actually, of course, Collier's work would not have made such a stir if it had not already been vaguely anticipated by a gradual change in social attitudes. Charles II had died in 1685; the so-called Revolution was bloodlessly effected three years later; and the decorous duet played by William and Mary proceeded to play tunes different from the roistering ditties which had previously echoed within Whitehall's precincts. The old careless expansiveness was on the way out; the voluntary closure of all save one theatre in London showed that the range of former playgoers was sadly declined; and among the new pieces produced – despite Congreve's triumphs in the nineties

– many exhibited a new, serious, and duller quality. These introduced features of a 'sentimental' and moralistic sort; and an early sign of the times appeared when William Wycherley, one of the masters of the comedy of manners, suddenly turned, in *The Plain Dealer* (1676), to lash out in anger at social hypocrisies and deceptions. A new mood clearly was at work.

This new mood, however, can hardly be considered either positive or creative, apt to inspire a fresh dramatic form: its spirit was born of repression. When the eighteenth century arrived there still remained a few dramatists, such as Sir John Vanbrugh and George Farquhar, who were able artistically to adjust the terms of the comedy of manners so as to suit the demands of a chastened social order: *The Confederacy* (1705), *The Beaux' Stratagem* (1707), and *The Recruiting Officer* (1706), plays which for long were popular and which even now yield delight, are sufficient indication of that. Other playwrights, notably Susannah Centlivre, found virtue in the style of 'Spanish intrigue' comedy which had been inherited from Beaumont and Fletcher. But for the most part the theatre during the first decades of the eighteenth century assumed a mongrel appearance, Collier's strictures having encouraged a false sobriety and yet the Restoration dramatists continuing to serve as models even although their gay and delicately poised wit was rapidly losing its sparkle. Not surprising is it to find that the single new experimental form arising out of this age was unashamedly mixed in character: John Gay's *The Beggar's Opera*, a great success in 1728 and still a lively entertainment, is of variegated origin and, despite the fact that it created a vogue for 'ballad opera', little or nothing truly vital ensued from it.

What does arouse a feeling of surprise, however, is a peculiar discrepancy amply evident when we turn from the earlier years of the century to the later, a discrepancy between actual dramatic achievement and the development of a novel critical approach towards the theatre, a critical approach indeed so fresh as to seem 'modern' in essence. In order to appreciate this aright we may begin by asking ourselves the same simple question which was asked concerning some previous periods: what plays from the second half of the eighteenth century have any vital interest for us today? The answer must be identical for each one of us: R. B. Sheridan's *The School for Scandal* (1777) certainly, and also, on a somewhat lower level, his *Rivals* (1775), *The Critic* (1779), and *The Duenna* (1775); Oliver Goldsmith's *She Stoops to Conquer* (1773) and, again somewhat lower, *The Good-Natured Man* (1768); these assuredly may be included in the list, and along with them there can be mentioned one or two other lesser works – *The Clandestine Marriage* (1766) by David Garrick and George Colman the Elder, the latter's *The Jealous Wife* (1761), and perhaps Frederick Reynolds' *The Dramatist* (1789). After these, what? Hardly anything: certainly none of the tragedies, whether those belonging to the long-established line of classical myth or, like Home's *Douglas* (1756), tentatively romantic; emphatically not the dull range of sentimental dramas turned out in the dozens by Richard Cumberland, Thomas Holcroft, Hugh Kelly, and their companions. Scores of these plays, in fact all of them are of interest to the student as records of a bygone era, but here our concern rests solely in such works as may have immediate pertinence to ourselves; and, in noting these few dramas, the poor grains sifted out of so much chaff, our first feeling of surprise comes from realizing that all the selected comedies in our list are written in styles which derive from the past; Sheridan's wit stems from the style of the seventeenth-century comedies of manners, and Goldsmith's humour derives ultimately from Shakespeare.

This element of surprise is accompanied by another. Towards the middle of the century, both in France and in England, the younger critics were beginning to evolve an anti-Aristotelian philosophy of the theatre; they wanted the 'natural' to be set upon the stage; interested in social betterment, they wanted serious drama to concern itself, not with the historical and mythical past, but with the ordinary men and women of their own day; and in comedy they wanted plays calculated less to entertain with laughter than to 'improve' with tears. And all they got was a series of boring or sensational scenes spread over a long line of plays from George Lillo's *The London Merchant* (1731) to Kelly's *False Delicacy* (1768). With something akin to shock we suddenly realize that the dullness so patent in the dramatic effort of these years was largely occasioned, not by any repressive control exercised by the Lord Chamberlain, but

by the critical and 'moral' theories enunciated by those belonging to the *avant-garde*.

In effect, however, it must be borne in mind that these
theories were intimately bound up with and indeed inspired by
the new spirit animating the auditorium. 'Sentimentalism' in all
its varying forms was then a pervasive force; both men and
women took delight in the luxury of pitying tears; and, as
Samuel Johnson well knew, in the theatre it is the audience that
calls the tune. Yet even those who called for scenes of pitiful
and sentimental import were conscious of the fact that these,
no matter how self-satisfying, could become boring if they were
not associated with something else; and as a result there came
into being the strange dichotomy which reigned in the playhouses of the middle and latter part of the eighteenth century.

This dichotomy expressed itself in two ways. In the first place
the dramatic offerings tended to split themselves into two quite
separate kinds. On the one hand there are the lachrymose
comedies and the pathetic tragedies; on the other there are the
innumerable 'shows' of all sorts, from farces to pantomimes,
which are so typical of this Georgian theatre. Both were combined in each evening's performance: tragedy was followed by
farce, farce by pantomime. These pantomimes bring us to the
second aspect of the dichotomy. The dullness of the tragedies
and of most of the comedies, together with the follies introduced into the majority of the pantomimes, did not mean that
the theatre had lost its vitality: on the contrary, the latter part
of the century was a period of very considerable playhouse
expansion in various directions. From about 1742 until 1776
David Garrick, internationally famous, ruled the stage, and
he was accompanied by numerous distinguished players; and
after his retirement there was no real vacuum, Sarah Siddons
and J. P. Kemble taking over his aegis. The art of acting was
now being savoured in a new way, and the general interest in
theatrical affairs is fully evidenced both by the space devoted
to these matters in contemporary periodicals and by an entirely new development – the launching of journals specifically
concerned with the playhouse. Constantly, too, thought and
effort were being devoted to the conditions of performance.
More and more attention was being given to scenic display,
and the public's interest in spectacle was markedly increased

when new methods of lighting the scenes were introduced by Garrick. And these developments were by no means confined to the metropolis. Throughout England these years witnessed a complete transformation in the status of the stage : instead of barns and outbuildings of local inns in which wandering strollers presented their wretched shows, Theatres Royal were being erected in most of the larger centres, and these were being conducted with a richness in display not unworthy of comparison with that operative in the two great patent houses, Drury Lane and Covent Garden, in London.

From one point of view we may look upon this enrichment of the scenic spectacle as resulting from the theatre's awareness of the inherent mediocrity of the age's comedies and tragedies; but from another point of view we may see here one of the conditions which contributed to the decline of the drama. Scenic spectacle can add much to the theatre, yet there are times when it can lead towards the stage's ruin. If it is associated with and designed to enhance a great play it possesses the power to intensify its appeal; if, as in this period, it remains a separate entity its influence can be destructive.

Everything, therefore, combined to thwart the efforts of the dramatists. No doubt few of them possessed any great potentialities, but even such limited talents as they possessed were crushed down by the conditions of the period. Although the objectives of the sentimental theorists were morally worthy and instinct with a desire to ameliorate social errors, their concepts tended to encourage the writing of tracts and to discourage the depiction of genuinely human characters. Although the stage made marked advances, these advances inclined towards concealing from audiences the poverty of the dramas being supplied by contemporary authors. The sorry fact remains that hardly a single one among the numerous plays written during the last years of the century could now be deemed wholly worthy of revival.

9

*The Reign
of Melodrama
and Extravaganza*

THE sentimental approach, often coloured by the tints of romanticism, endured throughout the greater part of the nineteenth century; but obviously the increasing circle of playgoers during those decades were not prepared to pay for their tickets in order to be bored, and very soon they began to ask for offerings more exciting than either the traditional 'tragedy' or the new sentimental drama could provide. In the major playhouses the skills and personalities of several prominent actors, assisted by the novel stage effects which could be achieved in houses illuminated by gas and equipped with machinery, certainly helped to keep many tedious pieces on the boards, and occasionally some bedraggled dramatic geese might even, by these means, be made temporarily to seem like swans; but basically this age is marked by a great cleavage between the 'legitimate' and the 'illegitimate' in drama, between the wearisome literary plays and the unashamedly 'theatrical' shows presented on the more popular stages.

If once again we ask ourselves the same kind of question we have asked before, only one answer can be expected or given. What plays of any intrinsic value to us come from the period which extends from 1800 to 1880? There may be a moment's pause, and then, hesitatingly, we say, "Tom Robertson's *Caste*", and there we stick.

This seems impossible. Rapidly we allow our minds to go over the dramatic works of the time. What about those hundreds of poetic dramas, several of them penned by writers of highest distinction? Hardly more than half a dozen can yield pleasure and profit even in the reading, none on the stage. Lord Byron's dramatic poems have vigour, yet they are far less powerful than his non-dramatic writings. Shelley's *Cenci* (1819)? Remembered less for any intrinsic merits than because we feel that its neglect might have been due to Victorian disapproval of its subject-matter. Talfourd's *Ion* (1836), once highly esteemed? A pretentiously uninteresting composition. Sheridan Knowles' shelf of tragedies and comedies? Worthy efforts, certainly, but lifeless. Robert Browning's array of dramas from *Strafford* (1837) to *Colombe's Birthday* (1844)? Even members of a Browning Society could not honestly recommend them to a theatre manager for revival. And so we go through the list on to the poetic plays of Lord Tennyson. But what about others not composed in verse? There is Lord Lytton's *Money* (1840), for example, and there is the *London Assurance* (1841) of Dion Boucicault: what of them? Nearer the mark, assuredly, yet we are bound to confess that, if they were to be revived today, even if skilled actors might bring some life to their lines, they could be looked upon only as period pieces. The thought of these plays, however, brings something else to our minds: we recall that Lytton's greatest success was *The Lady of Lyons* (1838), that Boucicault's was *The Colleen Bawn* (1860); and these, in turn, evoke a memory of Tom Taylor's *The Ticket-of-Leave Man* (1863). We fully realize that we have now come far down from the rarefied air of poetic heights, but at the same time we feel that we are here in contact with something that at least has liveliness – and suddenly we add to our previous brief answer, "And of course there were the melodramas."

Of course, there were the melodramas, the theatre's protest against the often excruciating dullness of the literary efforts. And, in turning to them, two further thoughts come to our minds – first, that the further we move from, let us say, *The Cenci* and the closer to *The Ticket-of-Leave Man* the more scenes we encounter invested not merely with theatrical vigour but also with a crude kind of stimulating interest, while, secondly, the less individual quality do we sense in the conception of the plays. A balance, therefore, must be maintained. Unquestionably the melodramatic pattern is inherently 'theatrical'; the very facts that the popular playhouses existed chiefly on this fare for so many years and that even the more distinguished houses came largely to depend on such works provide sufficient proof of that. In so far, therefore, the development of this form of entertainment during the earlier part of the nineteenth century was a welcome and healthy sign. On the other hand, this melodramatic pattern, apart from being crude, did not encourage much distinction between play and play: we speak of 'Victorian melodramas' in a manner different from that in which we refer to 'Greek tragedies'; the latter term suggests a series of plays each of which is unique and separate from the others although all of them belong to a general form and are moulded in a characteristic manner; in using the former term we evoke an image of hundreds upon hundreds of pieces fundamentally alike in planning and in composition. In general, one melodrama differs from another only in so far as its setting is concerned: one may be placed romantically in a pseudo-medieval environment where the Villain is a gloating baron, the Heroine a fair village girl, and the Hero a handsome young merchant; in another, amid supernatural wonders, the Villain may be an evil magician; and in still another, with scenes supposed to be naturalistic-realistic, a dark-faced, sneering landlord may pursue and persecute beautiful rustic innocence defended by a brave youth in contemporary attire.

We must, accordingly, look at both sides of the coin. The Victorian melodramas, while they were vigorously theatrical and while we can still occasionally enjoy their crude excitements, did not include among their massive bulk any plays possessing an individual quality which might distinguish them from others. One author might be more skilled in the devising of theatrical suspense; another might be a slightly better writer of dialogue than his companions; still another might be clever enough to discover a new milieu hitherto unexploited on the stage; but beyond this we cannot go. On the other hand, the melodramatic form was destined to exercise its power long after the *Sweeny Todds* and the *Nights in a Bar Room* had vanished from the playhouses. The success of Rudolf Besier's *The Barretts of Wimpole Street* in 1930 came from that author's adroitness in giving interesting dialogue and personality to a theme in which the Hero, a poet, rescues a fair reclining Heroine, a poetess, from the gloom of a Wimpole Street dungeon wherein she had been immured by a novel kind of Villain, her own father; and even today this melodramatic story, in musical shape, still makes its appeal. Nor does Besier's drama by any means stand alone: similar transmutations constantly confront us. If we may take an American example, Lillian Hellman's *The Children's Hour* seemed, in 1934, a daring, penetrating, and essentially novel dramatic achievement, but, without detracting in any way from its quality, we may admit that its theatrical appeal largely depended upon the fact that it was astutely cast in a melodramatic mould in which there appeared a yet newer type of Villain, a vicious little schoolgirl.

Much the same may be said of those 'extravaganzas' which in the nineteenth century were the fantastically comic counterpart of the melodramas. Such pieces, written in scores by J. R. Planché, H. J. Byron, and the Brothers Brough, may sadly be lacking in the fine precision of Congreve's wit, yet it is impossible to escape being impressed by their boisterous, vivacious exuberance. No doubt puns are most deplorable, and the puns which spurt and splutter in almost every line of every extravaganza exceed all possible allowances; yet in a period when dramatic dialogue in more literary comedies had become fatiguing and ineffective, they kept at least some liveliness on the boards.

10

The Modern Drama : i

THE FIRST
MOVEMENT

Pinero, Jones, and Wilde

ROBERTSON's *Caste* (1867) was almost the only play of permanent interest which we could think of as having come from the first eight decades of the nineteenth century, and this play, although it has been successfully revived in recent years, cannot be claimed to be an accomplished masterpiece. While it possesses some inherent merit, in the main its chief interest for us arises from its being a prime example of the new social realism which Robertson sought to bring within the theatre's walls. Already in the eighteenth century, of course, the cult of the 'natural' had been freely encouraged, and, as has been seen, there were several theatrical enthusiasts at that time who demanded that the stage should deal with current social problems. In their own time, however, this produced nothing save sentimental platitudes and moralizations, while during succeeding years the continuing cult of naturalism rarely got beyond the crude introduction of 'real' objects on the stage – live geese in a farmyard scene, a real lamp-post in the scene of a street. It should be remembered that in the earlier decades these objects usually appeared in the midst of a completely unrealistic setting constructed by means of wings and backdrops, so that they remained distinct from their surroundings. In so far as the content of the plays was concerned, it is true that the domestic kind of melodrama occasionally utilized social evils as plot elements – the miseries of rack-rented tenants, for example, or the temptations of the bar-room – and it is also true that one or two authors, such as Lytton in his *Money*, selected themes of immediate current interest. All of this, however, was purely tentative, and generally it was swamped by artificialities.

The significance of *Caste* is that Robertson consciously aimed at a complete change both in play and in stage representation. In the setting he sought for as much 'reality' as was possible, so that an interior should be constructed with walls, not open wings; his stage doors, fitted with proper knobs, had to look like ordinary solid doors, his windows had to be made like ordinary windows, his chairs and divans and tables had to be such as might be found in an actual room. Correspondingly, in the structure of his plays he endeavoured not only to reflect as faithfully as he could the 'real' speech and manners of his fictional characters, but also to illuminate his plots by making each one deal with a selected social topic or problem: thus in *Caste*, his first significant drama, the story, apart from its own interest, both exemplified and was enriched by the larger concept of class distinction. Robertson was no great genius and, like all pioneers, he had to spend so much energy in the process of reformation that his own works suffered, but unhesitatingly we can say that he was a man of talent and insight and that his efforts, even although he was not immediately companioned by other playwrights with similar aims, made a definite mark on the English stage.

In considering his objectives and achievements against the current playhouse procedure of his time we can see clearly that, although *Caste* proved a great success and although Robertson himself was encouraged to follow it with a series of plays conceived in the same manner, the age was not yet pre-

H

pared for any widespread revolution. That had to wait for nearly twenty years. When the revolution did come, by a strange coincidence it took shape amid surroundings which closely patterned the conditions operative in the Elizabethan period: this revival, like that with which Shakespeare had been associated, expressed itself during a period which marked both the close of a century and the end of a great Queen's reign; it, too, was heralded by premonitory signs; and it possessed the same potent force to develop and expand in scope, producing, as its predecessor had done, not merely one limited form (such as, for example, the Restoration comedy of manners) but a number of varyingly different styles and modes. What must firmly be kept in mind is that this was indeed a true revolution and that to its explosive force our own latest modern drama belongs; to ignore this can result only in a distorted view of present-day achievements.

In effect, therefore, we must now turn from a consideration of the furthest frontier of the theatrical waste land to a consideration of its frontier closest to us. Those who have placed the former towards the time of Shakespeare's retirement, those who have found it in the year when the Puritans closed the play-houses, and those who have been prepared to put the blame on the Licensing Act of 1737 are all, in general, agreed in treating the latter frontier as marked by the year 1956. According to that view, then, the waste land carried its aridness on through the whole of the first half of the present century – and it is precisely this assumption which now we are forced to examine, and such an examination can obviously not be adequately pursued without an objective scrutiny of the facts.

Although of course it is impossible to work out any theatrical movement into segments with absolutely precise chronological beginnings and ends, the general pattern of development from the last decades of the nineteenth century, when viewed from today's vantage in time, can hardly be questioned. (a) From about 1890, or a few seasons before, on to the opening years of the twentieth century, there is manifest the first revolutionary movement, with Sir Arthur Pinero, H. A. Jones, Oscar Wilde, and the Savoyards as its prime masters. (b) A new movement, with an excited medley of widely divergent styles and aims, made its appearance shortly after 1900 and, although seemingly broken by the impact of the First World War, continued its force until about 1930. (c) Once more a fresh impetus, again apparently broken by another war, carried on for a period of some twenty-five years. (d) And finally this ceded place to what we now call the 'contemporary'. Each of these four periods has its own characteristic features, yet when we look at them carefully we can see that they all belong to one dominant dramatic impetus: the second movement may give us the impression of having been animated wholly by reaction against the first, the third against the second, and the very latest against the third, but when we penetrate more deeply we are compelled to recognize that the driving power behind them was all the same.

At the very start, naturally, we must examine the beginning of the revolution, and here we realize that, like the Elizabethan revolution exactly three centuries previously, it inexplicably summoned forth the independent talents of many men: within a period of only three years, from 1892 to 1895, appeared Pinero's victorious *The Second Mrs Tanqueray,* Jones' *The Triumph of the Philistines,* Wilde's *Lady Windermere's Fan,* and G. B. Shaw's *Candida.* Thus the stage was completely new-set. In speaking of these three years, however, we must not forget that already in the eighties the tip of the revolution's long shadow had been thrown forward across the theatres: *The Mikado* was presented in 1885; the same year saw the *première* of Pinero's delightful farce, *The Magistrate*; two years later came his *Dandy Dick,* while three years previously Jones had won considerable acclaim for *The Silver King. The Mikado* and its companion operas were teaching men afresh the delights of stylistic wit, the farces were showing them how to laugh in a new way, and *The Silver King* was suggesting how the old melodrama could be wrought to new ends.

Quite obviously, within this realm we do not need to hesitate in our selection of plays interesting because of their novelty and valuable because of their stage worthiness. In general Pinero may seem to us now somewhat old-fashioned in his technique and over-intent upon the theme of the lady with a past, yet if we ignore the skill exhibited in *The Second Mrs Tanqueray* we do so at our peril; such a play as *The Thunderbolt* (1908) may not appear to be a very deep sociological study, but its seriousness of purpose does not entirely vanish on the modern stage; and even if we think that few others among his serious dramas bear present-day revival hardly anyone would be prepared to deny the thoughtfully comic vigour of *Trelawny of the 'Wells'* (1898). Jones' preoccupation with religious problems may not make particular appeal to us, but *Mrs Dane's Defence* (1900) is a magnificent example of taut structure and effectively economic dialogue. Wilde's epigrammatic dexterity in the four plays which ended with the delightfully fantastic *Importance of Being Earnest* (1895) needs no laudatory exposition; and who does not esteem the quality of *Widowers' Houses* (1892), *Mrs Warren's Profession* (1892), *Arms and the Man* (1894), *The Devil's Disciple* (1897), and *Caesar and Cleopatra* (1899)? So far, red-bearded G.B.S., with his infectious Irish brogue, had not succeeded in dominating the literary scene; on the other hand the fact that these plays had all been written before 1900 fully testifies to the strength inherent in the theatre during those last years of the nineteenth century. And, since the playhouse rightly has an extensive range, perhaps we ought not to turn up our noses even at Brandon Thomas' *Charley's Aunt* (1892) and Sir Charles Hawtrey's *The Private Secretary* (1883) — plays which confessedly are without any purpose save the adroit giving of delight, but possessing a theatrical appeal which has retained its potency.

To a large extent it may be said that this first revolutionary movement was founded on a rediscovery of lively and emphatic stage dialogue and of the means by which character might be presented. The language used in the melodramas, apart from being stereotyped, was for the most part penned by men who made few pretensions to literary quality; Robertson had exhibited more of an individual style, but even his dramatic speech lacked real distinction and soon came to seem old-fashioned: now, however, the actors were being supplied, not simply with hurriedly prepared texts, but with dramas seriously wrought — and the authors of these dramas regarded their work as sufficiently important to warrant publication in a form which might yield interest to a still wider reading public. Thoroughly characteristic is the invention during those years of stage-directions which went beyond the strict limits of the stage itself, providing a kind of narrative calculated to make the dialogue of interest even to those who had not had the opportunity of seeing the plays in action. Hitherto the literary and the theatrical had tended to remain distinct from each other, whereas during the last two decades of the nineteenth century they inclined to draw together, and consequently the basis for future endeavours was being surely laid.

If the plays of the immediate past had rarely displayed dialogue of a distinguished kind they had also failed to present individually interesting dramatic characters. In general the persons brought upon the boards had been artificially conceived and inexpertly presented. Although an actor such as Sir Henry Irving could thrill his audiences by the sheer force of his own strange personality, yet even his skill could not conceal the poverty of the material with which he had to work. Not surprisingly, therefore, the new dramatists applied themselves primarily to the creation of characters more subtly and more intensely imagined. And they found that in this attempt they required also to pay fresh attention to the manner in which these characters were put in action. Hence the Pineros and the Joneses concentrated a large part of their attention upon the fashioning of stories well and effectively told.

In these plays, we must confess, there was comparatively little of a sense of social purpose. Bernard Shaw, it is true, was struggling to bring the play of ideas into the theatre, but before 1900 he had not attracted much attention and, when we look around, we realize that in this sphere he stood almost alone. Although many works of the time touched upon the weaknesses of contemporary society, usually these weaknesses were dealt with in terms which affected individuals only: of a wider social reforming zeal very little is to be seen. The foundation built during those years was absolutely necessary, and without it the drama could not have made its further advances: nevertheless, we need not wonder that the next movement in the modern drama took shape as a revolution inside a revolution, with concentration upon social problems, and with experiments in technical variations.

11

The Modern Drama : ii

THE SECOND MOVEMENT

Galsworthy, the Repertory Playwrights, and G.B.S.

THE autonomy and distinctive nature of the second movement, extending over the first three decades of the present century, is marked in various ways. This was the period when fresh forces, from within and from without, wrought an entirely new pattern in stage affairs. During the eighties and nineties of the preceding century the playhouse realm had been characterized by the predominance of actor-managers in London, by the virtual extinction of the provincial stock companies outside of the metropolitan area, and by the strong rivalry of the music-halls which had created a mighty empire out of very humble beginnings. Before the twentieth century had made even a few short paces forward, however, a novel invention called the "Bioscope" made its appearance. Although insignificant at first, with only a few men dimly sensing what it might ultimately become, very soon the silent screen had attracted so much popular favour as to warrant the erection of ornate Picture Palaces, and as a result, within the space of a very few years, the throne of the music-hall Empires was doomed. From the theatre's point of view this seemed all to the good: the power of a powerful rival was being broken, and men confidently declared that a silent screen could not hope to vie seriously with the attractions of the stage.

Nevertheless, despite the gradual vanishing of the great rival, all did not seem so rosy as might have been expected. Outside of London the managers of the numerous Theatres Royal had become little more than booking agents for London touring companies, so that the 'provinces' were rendered devoid of independent theatrical activities. In London itself it is true that the actor-managers had been taught to accept plays written in the new styles made popular by Pinero and Jones, but already the revolutionary movement was taking further strides and these earlier styles were beginning to appear rather stale. Among those who belonged to the *avant-garde* there was accordingly an anxious search for the devising of fresh opportunities whereby still newer styles might be encouraged and demonstrated. Hence the development before 1914 of something absolutely novel – the establishment of dozens of theatre societies and play-producing clubs, together with the first approaches towards the building up of a 'repertory' movement. The seasons conducted by Harley Granville-Barker and J. E. Vedrenne at the Court Theatre between 1904 and 1907 proved to be as stimulating as George Devine's ventures at the same playhouse within recent years; Miss Annie Horniman created dramatic history by her support of the Manchester repertory theatre and Dublin's Abbey; a repertory company was founded in Glasgow; and just before the outbreak of war the first playhouse specifically built for repertory purposes was completed at Birmingham.

During the war, of course, these efforts were sadly interrupted, but immediately after the armistice they were caught up again with fresh enthusiasm – indeed with greater enthusiasm because at that time so many of the commercial houses were being given over to revues and musical comedies. The drama was now become a subject of eager interest; and the publication of numerous anthologies of new plays, of critical-historical surveys of the 'modern drama', of volumes discussing novel experiments in theatrical architecture and practice are a true mirroring of the spirit informing those years. This, then, was a period of excitement when all sorts of things previously undreamed of were being fervidly discussed. The ideas of Gordon Craig, the colour, vitality, and technical brilliance of the Russian Ballet, constructivism, impressionism, expressionism, all sparkled with a golden gloss. And with them came a stimulating sense of social purpose, with claims that the stage should explore both fresh forms and fresh ideological aims. Suddenly the theatre's horizons had become almost unbelievably extended.

What did this expansion produce?

In seeking an answer to this question one rather surprising thing immediately becomes apparent. If the young enthusiasts of the period had been asked what, in their view, was the most important theatrical force of their age and the one likeliest to endure, we may be reasonably certain that before 1914 the majority would immediately have spoken in elated terms about the grim regional drama being cultivated by the 'repertory' authors, as exemplified in such plays as Elizabeth Baker's *Chains* (1909) or St John Ervine's *Jane Clegg* (1913), while after 1918 the stress would have been laid on expressionistic and other experiments exemplified in plays such as C. K. Munro's *Rumour* (1922). Yet these are precisely the dramas which are now largely forgotten or, if remembered, ignored; we may freely acknowledge the integrity of purpose which inspired most of them, and at the same time recognize that almost all of them are dated. The only 'regional' dramatic movement which succeeded in producing any true masterpieces was that centred in Dublin – and obviously, although the term 'regional' may be used legitimately here in an historical sense, in a larger sense it is manifestly incorrect. Thanks to W. B. Yeats and J. M. Synge this movement, in spite of its intense concentration upon the local scene, found both broader themes and a richer, more imaginative, form of expression than was to be discovered elsewhere: the vision which invests *In the Shadow of the Glen* (1903), *Riders to the Sea* (1904), and *The Playboy of the Western World* (1907) had, moreover, a continuing impulse. Sean O'Casey's *Juno and the Paycock* (1925) and *The Plough and the Stars* (1926) were fed from the same source – and incidentally it may be observed that this author, after he had left Ireland, was virtually the only dramatist writing in English who succeeded in mastering the expressionist style: his *Silver Tassie* (1929) may have been a failure in its own time, but the guess might be hazarded that if it were to be revived now it might appear to have been the most unduly neglected achievement of its generation.

Another peculiar thing is that the 'commercial' playwright who came closest to the spirit animating the 'repertory' authors found himself able far better than they to create works which come near to having real value for us now. Although John Galsworthy's reputation has seriously fallen during these our latter days and although his writings are hardly known to the contemporary stage, another guess might be hazarded – that, if one of his better plays were now to be given a full-scale revival, it would mean much more to us than any of the once-lauded creations of the Lancashire school. He wrote story-plays – admitted; he fashioned them largely within the framework established by Pinero – admitted; his style was straightforward and perhaps lacking in variety – also admitted; but, after offering these adverse criticisms, we find ourselves compelled to acknowledge that he was in essence more Brechtian than Brecht in his basic approach to the stage. Brecht preached that audiences should be exposed to a theatrical scene exhibiting some prime action of social significance and that the author should stimulate them to think for themselves about this action, in the hope that their thoughts would finally move them to action. The famous concept of 'alienation', therefore, implies two things – that the spectators should not become emotionally involved in the play presented before them and that they should be encouraged to remain critically alert to form their own conclusions concerning the significance of the events enacted on the stage. As a matter of fact, however, in most of his writings for the theatre Brecht left his spectators in no doubt as to what he believed their thoughts ought to be : by the use of placards and songs and loaded character delineations he stressed the particular way in which he wanted each of his dramas to be interpreted. Thus there exists a wide discrepancy between his theoretical concept and his theatrical practice. Galsworthy's method, on the other hand, is honestly designed to stimulate thought; since he was a burning humanitarian, he cannot — and indeed he does not wish to — conceal from us his sense of personal indignation at abuses or his rage at the malpractices of social life, yet at the same time his case is put before us with controlled austerity, and for that very reason it often becomes the more powerful. Amid all the twentieth-century plays of revolutionary intent almost the only one which resulted in the immediate political reformation of a dark cruelty was *Justice* (1910). Why? Because the author, deeply as he felt about the imposition of solitary confinement, refused to dictate and permitted his audiences to judge for themselves. Here, and in his other dramas, appear no melodramatic villains; no caricatures are permitted to intrude, there are no vitriolic outbursts of wrath.

This is not said to suggest that Galsworthy's plays call imperiously for present-day revival: their patterns maybe are too old-fashioned for that, and their style too closely adjusted to the reality of their own time. It may, however, justifiably be claimed that a sympathetic appreciation of his methods and of his approach might be a salutory experience for dramatic writers of today. He was a revolutionary fired by no self-interest, driven forward by no feeling of personal injustice, and, even when he was most moved to indignation, preserving his sense of balance.

Some attempts have been made of late to rehabilitate a playwright less apt to be troubled by contemplation of concrete social injustices, more inclined to deal with the pressures upon individuals of the social conventions surrounding them; but strangely the dramatic writings of this man, Harley Granville-Barker, in spite of his wide experience as actor and director, seem too subtle for the stage. His treatment of group-scenes is magnificent, showing the hand of a true master: a recent revival of *The Voysey Inheritance* (1905) has demonstrated both his agility of mind and his keenly observant eye; nevertheless, his work as a whole leaves us vaguely dissatisfied — even *Madras House* (1910) fails completely to hold us, while amid the scenes of *The Secret Life* (1923) we wander in puzzlement. Although this author unquestionably did much to refine, deepen, and intensify realistic dramatic dialogue, he was not able, with all his practical stage experience, to find adequate form for his imaginative visions. More immediately successful, within his chosen field, was another playwright, Somerset Maugham, who very nearly succeeded in establishing a different kind of theatre which might be described as a modern comedy of manners with overt social implications; unfortunately, however, as we look back now, we realize that he, too, largely failed. Although *The Circle* (1921) is a piece of brilliantly simple architectural form and although for its own time its dialogue was perfectly poised, in present-day revival its incisiveness is apt to vanish, its action seems artificially contrived and even trite: little is evident of the elusive quality that has kept Congreve's plays alive.

In the last analysis adequate dramatic form was achieved at this period only by two men – the one an ebullient Irishman, George Bernard Shaw, and the other a retiring, introverted Scotsman, Sir James Barrie. In our age, an age of violence, it might have seemed as though the latter's quiet sentimentalism could not possibly make any appeal, and of course in its more blatant manifestations (*Mary Rose* (1920), for example) it does not. At the same time no one can fail to recognize and admire the delicate subtlety of his craftsmanship, the precision of his observing eye, the subdued understatement of his humorous fancy, the skill with which he exhibits his sadly resigned and yet fundamentally comic contemplation of life. Here was a writer who won contemporary acclaim for a long series of plays from the immortal dream-world of *Peter Pan* (1904), the topsiturviness of *The Admirable Crichton* (1902), and the penetration of *What Every Woman Knows* (1908), on to the enchanted magic of *Dear Brutus* (1917); and here was an artist who not only can still profitably be studied by today's playwrights but can also, in revival, capture the attention and esteem of even the unwilling and reluctant.

Clearly, however, the man who stands out above all his companions is the flamboyant Bernard Shaw, and the period between 1900 and 1930 distinctively belonged to him. Before the beginning of the century he was known only to a very limited circle; by the year 1905 he was the central dramatist in the Vedrenne-Barker repertory season at the Court, and in 1929, the first British dramatic festival, for which he wrote *The*

Apple Cart, was dedicated to him. Despite the fact that only a few years ago (in 1962, to be exact) he was being described as a dramatist who has dropped out of the theatre and as one who cannot bear comparison with Ben Jonson, recent theatrical productions have demonstrated that he is as alive today as he was during those eventful decades half a century ago; and even so we must be careful to avoid being misled by the use of that phrase 'dropped out': actually, as both theatrical productions and publications of his writings amply demonstrate, he has never ceased to appeal.

Among the various editions of his literary work the 'Plays' and the 'Prefaces' are currently to be seen on booksellers' shelves in two bulky collected volumes, and this separation of his dramatic from his non-dramatic prose not only appears to be fully justified but also to symbolize the form of his impact upon the twentieth-century public. The prefaces, of course, originally were issued as lengthy introductions to the various plays, and it is common to think of the drama and its introduction as single complete wholes: when, however, we look at them in disjunction we may well be inclined to observe considerable discrepancies between them – and the reason for this is not far to seek. From the very beginning of his lengthy career Shaw was an eager social reformer, an enthusiastic if eccentric admirer of Ibsen, a revolutionary who loved to shock by means of bold paradox. Almost every one of his plays, therefore, resulted from serious thought and wide perusal of works – historical, sociological, and philosophic – related to its central theme. In the prefaces the process of that thinking and reading is revealed in vigorous critical prose, and, this being so, clearly a careful examination of the preface to each play is essential for an understanding of the drama to which it is attached. Nevertheless, the more we examine them, the more we come to realize that in essence they are distinct, each having its own form and worth, and that often the one leads towards a different intellectual and emotional experience from that which arises from the other. This double effect is consequent upon the obvious facts that in the composition of his prefaces Shaw was fundamentally intent upon the exposition of facts and ideas and that in his best plays he became basically a dramatist, a writer almost completely gripped and controlled by the theatrical impulse. Quite frequently, therefore, the impression with which we are left at the close of a performance of one of his plays differs subtly from our appreciation of the arguments presented in its attached preface. A full understanding of the double process may possibly be demonstrated best by a comparison. If we turn, for instance, to Charles Morgan's explicative introduction to his *The Burning Glass* (1954), we feel at first that we have before us an example of the 'Shavian' procedure: penetrating further, we sense a wide distinction between the writings of these two authors; we find ourselves deeply moved by the strength, intensity, and skilful exposition displayed in Morgan's prefatory essay, and, when we move on to the drama we see that it indeed is a direct and faithful dramatic presentation of the theme and the ideas which had been so excellently argued in the introduction. Precisely because of this, however, *The Burning Glass* as a play remains disappointing – certainly not a failure, but lacking independent vitality and theatrical incisiveness. While it cannot be said that in composing any of his dramas Shaw forgets what he had written in the preface, unquestionably the theatre-man in him is almost wholly in control: and this means that frequently he allows his own central idea to be sacrificed or modified by his inherent interest in dramatic effect: as he himself has said, Harlequin is for ever standing in the wings of his theatre of the imagination, for ever ready to make an unexpected, improvised leap over the boards – and Harlequin can play havoc with ideas.

Because of this, Shaw the dramatist follows no doctrinaire method; like some fleeting will o' the wisp, he continually eludes capture; he cannot be pinned down as a specimen for a critical cabinet. At moments he seems to be the avowed enemy of the well-made play, the exponent of the conversation-piece and the drama of ideas. Yet it is not hard to recognize his inner awareness of the virtues of the well-made play and his willingness to utilize its technique, whenever it suits him, for his own purposes. Similarly he always refused – or found himself refusing – to be bound in his dramatic dialogue within the terms of his admired Ibsen. The range of his characters' utterances is always basically theatrical: its rhythms and its sentence patterns, of course, are characteristically his own, just as, let us say, Shakespeare's speech belongs to himself, yet it freely adapts itself to

wellnigh everything from the seriousness of a Major Barbara
to that of a Lilith, from the exuberance of a Jack Tanner to
that of his spiritual ancestor Don Juan.

Shaw's plays, therefore, although they spring ultimately from
philosophical and sociological cogitations, are written with the
object of interesting and entertaining audiences in the playhouse. He may take delight in shocking and startling the spectators, but rarely does he do this without a twinkle in his eye
or even without an implied laugh at himself: even at his most
seriously philosophic, he is hardly ever solemn: he sets out to
surprise his public, he never feels inclined to insult them.

As may well be understood, Shaw's levity, his refusal to be
bound by critical theories, his constant aiming at entertainment,
have tended to estrange him somewhat from the school of more
serious and embittered playwrights of recent years; he himself
honestly believed in the power of verbal communication, and,
even if for a moment, when writing *Back to Methuselah* (1919–
20), he descended into the dark vale of anti-human pessimism,
he still maintained at least a glimmer of hope and sought for a
possible upward path. No doubt, like all masters – and Shaw
was a playwright of masterly power – he was not always able
to achieve perfection; no doubt his sense of the ludicrous occasionally led him towards penning trivialities, even worthless
absurdities: on the other hand an author deserves to be judged
by his best work, and the best work of G.B.S. has a command,
an assurance, a liveliness which go far beyond anything contributed later to the theatre. Even if he had stood alone in his
period, which he does not, his plays would be sufficient in themselves to disprove the statement that the year 1956 witnessed
the first revival of British playwriting since Shakespearian times.
In seeking for the inception of such a revival we must find it in
the movement which began, with Shaw as one of its participants, within the last twenty years of the nineteenth century,
and which still is operative. *Widowers' Houses, Mrs Warren's
Profession, The Man of Destiny, Caesar and Cleopatra,
Candida, The Devil's Disciple* – written during the earlier decades; *Man and Superman, Major Barbara, The Doctor's Dilemma, Pygmalion, Androcles and the Lion* – produced within
the years preceding the outbreak of the First World War; *Heartbreak House, Back to Methuselah,* and *Saint Joan* – appearing

immediately after the cessation of hostilities; even *In Good King Charles's Golden Days, The Apple Cart,* and *Too True to be Good* – his latest experiments : all these combine as one mighty achievement, to ignore the value of which may be regarded as a self-revealing confession.

12

The Modern Drama : iii

THE THIRD MOVEMENT

Bridie, Priestley, Eliot, and Fry

SHAW's latest writings came after 1930, and thus this man, who had started his dramatic career during the first movement of the revolutionary theatre and who dominated the second, was able at least to cross the threshold of the third movement, that which lay within the twenty-five years from 1930 to 1955.

So far as the physical conditions of the playhouse and its surroundings were concerned, this period witnessed many changes. In 1927 the silence of the film was shattered by the raucous recording of Al Jolson's voice, and with unexpected suddenness the 'talking pictures', accompanied by the rapid growth of the 'wireless drama', became one of the most significant forces separating the years 1930 onward from the preceding three decades of the century. Soon, too, the 'talking pictures' discovered how to give colour to their black-and-white images, allowing them to vie with, and indeed to surpass, anything that the stage could offer in spectacular display. For vast numbers of spectators, accordingly, the word 'theatre' came to mean the place where films were shown, and the old theatre, ever more and more compelled to make use of the epithet 'living', was confronted by a menacingly gigantic rival. As a result of this the twenty-five years from 1930 to 1955 saw the culmination of a movement which had been pursuing its materially destructive career all through the earlier decades of the century : during the course of those fifty years hundreds of playhouses throughout the country were ruthlessly torn down or adapted to other than theatrical use. Against such a dismal picture, however, must be set another – a picture showing an absolutely fresh development which, for England, might almost be styled unbelievable: the public, hardly realizing what was happening, was persuaded to accept a novel proposition, that, whether they were playgoers or not, some of their tax-money should go towards patronage of the playhouse. Although the fuller story of this innovation, with its symbolic establishment of a National Theatre, may best be left over for consideration when the New Wave is being examined, at least its first general results need to be observed here. During the earlier years repertory enthusiasts had had to rely upon either donations from such persons as might be induced to contribute their small sums to assist a common cause or upon the munificence of an Annie Horniman and a Barry Jackson. By 1955 not only was the Arts Council handing out Treasury money to companies both in London and in regional centres, but also several municipal authorities, albeit with some initial puzzled reluctance, were beginning to consider the assignment of rate-payers' cash to local civic ventures. Nor was this material change unheralded; for at least two decades before 1955 numerous enthusiasts were clearly beginning to discuss the idea of a National Theatre and of civic theatres not just as a dream but as an impending reality.

Amid these conditions a new kind of dramatic impulse becomes evident during the thirties. Although we are confronted here with a wide variety of different sorts of theatrical endeavour, we get the impression that the prevailing trend was towards the cultivation of what may be called 'style': not without significance is the fact that the most characteristic actor of the period was John Gielgud, an artist for whom 'tradition' and 'style' were all-important. Equally characteristic was the work of those playwrights who inclined either towards an imaginative and even formalized use of the older realism or towards a breaking-away from the realistic trammels through the pursuit of historical themes and of themes fantastically conceived and through explorations within the realm of the poetic theatre.

None of these things, of course, were entirely novel. The mistaken excitement over Stephen Phillips' *Paolo and Francesca* in 1902 had been generated by a largely unconscious desire to welcome the poetic, and the same may be said about the reception of J. E. Flecker's *Hassan* some twenty years later. On the other hand those who applied themselves to the writing of such plays – Gordon Bottomley, Lascelles Abercrombie, even John Masefield – generally found themselves compelled to orient their dramas in the direction of the amateur acting companies. The historical trend, it is true, had had a somewhat happier fate: several of Shaw's plays, including *Saint Joan,* took their material from the past, and proved successful; John Drinkwater won universal applause for his *Abraham Lincoln* in 1918; and numerous other similar plays could be listed which gained at least modified acclaim. As a whole, however, these efforts were swamped under the crushing weight of the prevailing realism, and in this they shared the fate of most of the dramas which sought to exploit the inner world of the imagination. No doubt all of them helped to lay the foundation, but after all, although every piece of architecture needs a firm basis, it is not of that basis we think as we look upon its completed structure.

The third period in the development of the modern drama did, of course, produce a rich and often effective series of 'straightforward' plays written, in the realistic mode, by such skilled authors as Emlyn Williams, A. J. Cronin, John van Druten, Terence Rattigan, and others; yet probably, when the time arrives for looking at this age in true historical perspective, its inner spirit will be seen reflected most emphatically and clearly in the works of James Bridie, J. B. Priestley, T. S. Eliot, Christopher Fry, and Noël Coward. Stress upon the qualifying adverb 'probably' is necessary here, since we are still too close in time for the reaching of any final judgment; nevertheless, if we do accept these authors as most representative of the driving force operative between 1930 and 1955, we must also be careful not to permit current prejudices to influence our assessment of their worth. These, we must remember, were the playwrights against whom the latest new wave of dramatists have revolted, and we must remember, too, that movements in the theatre are often apt to resemble changes in fashion: when a new mode is introduced yesterday's clothes frequently seem to be more antiquated than those belonging to a distant past, so that the designers may be prepared to imitate or, with modifications, to exploit the styles of by-gone decades even while they have nothing but contempt for what was being worn the day before. We ought, therefore, in trying to estimate the value of the dramas produced between 1930 and 1955 to remain alert to the possibility that a future dramatic development may well result in carrying us back to a fresh appreciation of their accomplishment.

Priestley's most popular contributions to the stage were the closest in form to the earlier realistic tradition, but his dramatic preoccupation with a fourth dimension and his delving into the subconscious set his works apart. Even in the midst of what appears on the surface to be an ordinary commonplace environment an eerie strangeness is invoked, sometimes muted as in *Dangerous Corner* (1932), sometimes philosophical as in *Time and the Conways* (1937), sometimes moving on to a world in which the 'real' is supplanted by complete unreality, as in *Johnson over Jordan* (1939), *They Came to a City* (1943), and *Dragon's Mouth* (1952).

While Priestley's distinctive quality rests in a determined sense of purpose, Bridie's depends upon an idiosyncratic elusiveness: sometimes he seems like a gnome who is for ever cocking a snook at us and for ever avoiding capture. And no doubt it is characteristic of the two men that whereas the former's plays are in general carefully planned and skilfully wrought, most of the latter's give the impression of flowing on without any obviously patterned course. Characteristic also is the fact that Bridie clearly finds his true natural habitat in the distantly set parable of *Tobias and the Angel* (1930), of the sweeping past-present-and-future of *A Sleeping Clergyman* (1933), and of *Mr Bolfry's* mingled reality and magic (1943).

Although neither of these authors can be described in any valid sense as an historical playwright or as one tending towards the poetic, they inhabit the world which produced and welcomed Clifford Bax's *The Rose without a Thorn* (1932), Gordon Daviot's *Richard of Bordeaux* (1932), Eliot's *Murder in the Cathedral* (1935), and, later, the triumphantly successful writings of Christopher Fry. In the poetic drama, the final victory over realism and naturalism, came the apotheosis of that sense of style which the age was seeking.

The trouble with the poetic drama is, obviously, that we live at present in a prosaic age. Shakespeare flourished during the time when the rich diapasons of the King James' Bible were not so far removed from the speech of ordinary life; our Bible is quite another kind of thing, scientifically aiming at exactitude in translation and stylistically commonplace. The power of poetry has departed from us; two or three years ago Cyril Connolly rightly observed that "there is now no poet under fifty who is famous, no poem since the Thirties which is a household word". Thus, whereas Shakespeare had firm ground under his feet, any twentieth-century playwright who essays the poetic form is driven to hack out his own path over quaggy ground. He can adopt one of only two possible procedures: either he has to acknowledge the absence of the poetic among us and elect to compromise, furtively trying to superimpose a poetic quality upon our dulled common utterance, or he has to attempt the difficult task of persuading the public to accept a speech-form of his own creation. Eliot's first play, *Murder in the Cathedral*, pursued the second course, but, after all, this play was designed for production in a church and not in a theatre. In his later works and in his critical pronouncements he turned back to the first alternative, concealing the 'poetic' element as much as he could, and, in *The Confidential Clerk* (1953) and *The Elder Statesman* (1958), even going so far as to suggest to the public that they were watching and listening to ordinary 'straightforward' dramas, realistic in concept and presentation.

Christopher Fry was bolder. He was prepared to offer no

concessions, and, when *The Lady's Not for Burning* (1948), *Venus Observed* (1950), and *Ring Round the Moon* (1950) captured the public, it looked as though the long, lonely efforts of Bottomley and Abercrombie had fully and finally found complete justification. The triumph, however, was not destined to last long. Only a few years were to elapse before a new school of playwrights directed their angry attack upon the stage which had welcomed this truly extraordinary development, many of them lumping together the 'well-made play', the 'poetic drama', and 'drawing-room comedy' indiscriminately into their buckets under the kitchen sink.

Reference to drawing-room comedy reminds us that Priestley, Bridie, Eliot, and Fry had one other lively partner — the irrepressible and inimitable Noël Coward, an actor-playwright who links together the second, third, and fourth movements in the growth of the modern drama and who conceivably may be regarded in the future as stepping over the threshold into a by no means impossible fifth period in its development. After the success of *The Young Idea* (1921), *The Vortex* (1924), *Hay Fever* (1925), *Easy Virtue* (1925), and with his display of virtuosity as author, composer, and producer of *Bitter Sweet* (1929), he became a prime symbol of the spirit of the twenties; the amazing diversity of his activities from the exhibition of elegance and wit in *Private Lives* (1930) and *Design for Living* (1932), through the historical sweep of *Cavalcade* (1931), on to the variegated texture of *To-night at 8.30* (1935) transformed him into a symbol of the thirties; in 1941 the airy *Blithe Spirit* and the delightfully charming *Present Laughter* of 1942 were confessedly composed in a mood which made him refuse to believe that he "belonged to a dying civilization"; and now, although his unrepentant faith in the theatre of entertainment made him anathema to many after 1956, he has suddenly come into his own again. The year 1964 saw a revival of *Hay Fever*; *Blithe Spirit*, in a musical version under the title of *High Spirits*, appeared almost at the same time in the West End; at least four of his earlier plays were to be seen on television screens; and he himself has delighted audiences in his own latest writings.

With him we may step forward over and across the dividing-line of the year 1956.

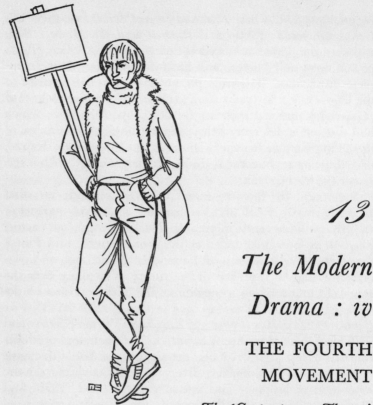

13

The Modern Drama : iv

THE FOURTH MOVEMENT

The 'Contemporary Theatre'

1956; The Royal Court Theatre; the 8th of May; John Osborne's *Look Back in Anger* – again and again it has been affirmed that the English drama was reborn with this *première*.

There is certainly no justification for minimizing the importance of the occasion. The excited reception of the play stands as a symbol, marking the start of a fourth movement in the development of the modern drama. Nevertheless, despite the significance of this production, a full understanding of its force depends upon an appreciation of the conditions amid which it came into being, conditions which have determined the characteristic forms of the contemporary theatre.

These conditions are diverse and distinct in kind, independent of each other; any single one of them would in itself have had a strong influence on theatrical activities; but their full power has come from the fact that they all reached their maturity about the same time, the early fifties of the century.

(i) First may be considered the popularization of television. As we have seen, the twenty years which saw the beginnings of the modern drama found the theatre confronted by a mighty rival in the music-hall; within the next three decades the silent film reached its final triumphs, crushing the music-hall's power in the process; once more, from about 1930 to the 1950's, the stage was menaced by another mighty rival, the 'talking-picture', which, obliterating the silent film and increasing its appeal when black-and-white images were transformed into images richly colourful, forced the theatre to emphasize its 'live' or 'living' quality and which caused it to look around for means whereby the challenge might be met. During that period the growth of the poetic drama may well be regarded as at least a partial reply to that challenge, the encouragement of plays uniquely characteristic of the 'living' playhouse and alien to the cinema's realm.

Then, to their dismay, the 'talking pictures' discovered that the kingdom they had set up was being threatened by a still later invention – the television screen. Just at first this came slowly, its progress hindered by war. In 1936 experimental two-hour programmes were transmitted daily; by 1939 interest in television was spreading beyond a narrow circle of enthusiasts; but naturally all that was suddenly stopped, and it was not until 1946 that a fresh start was made. Even then the movement forward was comparatively slow: as late as 1953, the year of the Coronation, hundreds of thousands of people had to flock to public bars and hotels if they wished to view the ceremonies. By 1955, however, the aerial masts had sprouted everywhere, and commercial television had been added to the BBC.

On the purely material level it would appear that this fresh kind of entertainment operated far less adversely upon the stage than upon the world of the screen. True, its programmes, added to those of the radio, offered the public another inducement for staying at home instead of expending money and energy in going to the theatre; but obviously what could be seen on the television screens was more akin to what might be seen on the cinema screens than to what was provided in the playhouses. Understandably, therefore, the former suffered more than the latter. And, indeed, at times the theatre found television even beneficial. It would seem that many potential filmgoers are tempted to remain at home with their television-sets instead of engaging in the trouble and expense of going out to a cinema; and it is obvious that, if the film companies were to allow their latest pictures to be televised, hardly any viewers would feel inclined to see these pictures again in an enlarged form; on the other hand, there appears to be sufficient evidence to prove that the televising of a play, whether in whole or in part, does have the effect of persuading some viewers to book tickets for a live performance. Still further, the presentation of specially prepared productions of stage plays, from those of Shakespeare to those of Maugham, Coward, and Shaw, has un-questionably brought to many an awareness of, and an interest in, the drama which otherwise they would have lacked.

Consideration of the material influence of television, how-ever, must be accompanied by consideration of influences more subtle and less easy to define and determine. One basic truth, of course, is that, although a stage production can be repro-duced on the home screens and although plays originally com-posed for television can later be given productions on the stage, the effects resultant from each are entirely different; and, since the effects are different, the two forms of drama must not be confused. This truth becomes particularly significant when we turn to examine what has been happening during the past ten or fifteen years.

During the days when the radio was the only available home entertainment and when the picture-house was the only potent rival of the stage, writers, both young and fully established, were commissioned to prepare short plays and sketches for the one and screen-plays for the other. The conditions imposed by the radio and by the cinema, however, were such as to force the writers to employ techniques entirely different from those proper to plays intended to be seen and heard by an audience: a 'wireless drama' might later be given representation in a theatre and a 'screen-play' might be adapted as a 'stage-play', but everyone knows that instances of such procedures are rare indeed. All of this means that the practice of writing playlets for the radio and the practice of composing screen-plays could have only slight effect upon ordinary playwriting.

Similar commissions were made by the BBC for their new medium, relatively few at the start but becoming more numerous in the early fifties and increasing markedly after the BBC and ITV began to compete with each other after 1955. Thus many more young authors found fresh opportunities, during their periods of apprenticeship, to earn their living, not by application to some distasteful tasks, but by engaging in work which offered them experience in planning situations and in writing dialogue; perhaps some of them were thus enabled to pursue a vocation which otherwise they might have been forced to abandon; and, since obviously the television-drama is more closely allied to stage-drama than to radio-drama, there was a general tendency to draw them all towards the theatre.

At first it might seem as though these new conditions, from the stage's point of view, were all to the good, but further consideration suggests that the relationship between television and theatre, between writing for the one and writing for the other, is by no means so simple. This subject, as yet not adequately studied, is in fact complex, and, although it would not be proper to attempt any discussion of it here, one of its aspects may be selected for brief mention. Obviously, a very common dramatic form called for in television programmes is the relatively short sketch, more or less equivalent to those 'one-acts' which, becoming popular during the eighteenth century, continued to be written by the score until the time came, towards the close of the nineteenth century, when 'curtain-raisers' were gradually dispensed with. We need not doubt that the present revival of interest in such short plays has been derived and encouraged by the demands of television. Now the history of the one-act play is by no means without distinction, and accordingly this fresh development of the form might be unreservedly welcomed were it not for two related considerations. The first of these is that practice in the composing of short pieces cannot always be regarded as the best training for a young dramatist: the normal stage-play is one which will run for about two hours and a half, sometimes a little less, sometimes more, and such a work demands larger architectural planning than can usually be learned in the writing of shorter pieces. The second consideration is that young dramatists may be confronted by an insidious temptation to take a short play originally conceived, whether by deliberation or not, within terms proper to television and spin it out until it reaches the limits of a full-length drama: such procedure may, of course, occasionally prove successful, but only too often we may get the impression of looking at a small cottage which has been sprawlingly extended.

In a period when firm dramatic forms and established technique are commonly accepted – as, for example, during the reign of the 'well-made' play – this would not matter; but in a time such as the present, when traditional methods have been set aside and there is anxious experimentation in fresh directions, experience in writing for a medium which, for all its apparent similarities, is distinct from the stage may contribute towards confusion.

(ii) The advent of television, then, must be seen as a potent force affecting contemporary drama in diverse ways, and with it may be associated the rediscovery of older stage forms and the invention of new ones. The 'well-made' play flourished in an age when virtually there was only one single type of theatre and one basic theatrical philosophy: the word 'theatre' meant the picture-frame structure, with the actors behind the footlights pretending to give the audience the illusion of reality. An awareness of other possibilities began to emerge towards the close of the nineteenth century and to be eagerly discussed during the first decades of our own century, but, although practical experiments were attempted in some other countries, stage productions in England kept mainly within traditional limits. The spectators certainly did have opportunities of witnessing scenes not accompanied by realistic settings and there were other departures from the familiar conventions; yet fundamentally the picture-frame stage maintained its dominance.

Very soon after the resumption of regular theatrical activities in 1945, however, eager debate was resumed, with the result that the concept of the open-stage, in all its varied forms, became the ideal. Although the older theatres remained, new ventures like the Mermaid and the Chichester playhouses, combined with the remodelling of proscenium-arch structures and with less restrained productional methods, brought a new spirit of freedom, excited novel ideas, aroused the desire to explore fresh styles. Freedom, however, while welcome, almost always carries with it its own problems; it certainly has acted as an inspiring force during the past ten years, but at the same time it has made the already complex conditions even more perplexing for younger dramatists in their search for appropriate dramatic forms.

(iii) Of still greater and more immediate significance is a third innovation, which, like the others, started in the forties and grew to vigorous adolescence in the early fifties. Already brief attention has been drawn to its beginnings, but now it requires rather more examination. Early in 1940 a group of enthusiasts, with the aid of small grants from the Pilgrim Trust and the Treasury, succeeded in launching CEMA, the Council for the Encouragement of Music and the Arts. Initially its object was a very simple one – to bring music and drama to the evacuation areas – and although its activities materially increased as London and other cities suffered from bombing, it remained an organization devoted to a particular war-time purpose. Nevertheless, its practical efforts were such as to suggest further possibilities, and in June 1945 the Arts Council of Great Britain took its place, determined to carry on its work in a larger way. Although for a long time the larger way resembled rather a widened country road than a great new trunk thoroughfare, soon fresh concepts and increased resources wrought a mighty change. The listing of monetary figures, even in summary form, is apt to be dull, but perhaps the most effective manner of demonstrating the scope of the Council's growth is to record that, whereas during its first financial year the total Treasury grant amounted to £175,000, three years later this sum had been increased to £428,000, in 1957 had risen close to the million mark, and in 1965 had reached more than three million : in 1945 less than £30,000 in grants and guarantees had been offered to theatrical ventures; in 1948 the corresponding expenditure was above £66,000; in 1957, even although £473,000 was assigned for opera and ballet, some £62,000 was divided among thirty theatre companies; the Council's Report for 1965 records the allotment of more than half a million to dramatic organizations and in the Report for 1967 an impressive graph shows an almost perpendicular line soaring upwards above the one-and-a-half million mark.

These figures amply prove that there was complete justification for the title given to the Council's Report for 1957–58 – "A New Pattern of Patronage".

They also justify the title-heading of the opening article in *The Stage Year Book* for 1965 – "The Two Theatres". In 1951 Bernard Miles established an Elizabethan-type Mermaid Theatre in St John's Wood; two years later Joan Littlewood's Theatre Workshop found a London home at the Theatre Royal, Stratford East; in 1956 the English Stage Company was established at the Royal Court; a new Mermaid Theatre in the City was opened in 1959; the Royal Shakespeare Company from Stratford-upon-Avon took over the Aldwych in 1961; and in 1963 the Old Vic became The National Theatre. Naturally, all of these vary considerably in management, in aim, and in achievement; but they stand together as organizations which could not have come into being or pursued their activities without external assistance and which, therefore, are distinct from the commercial West End playhouses. Nor do they remain alone. The Arts Council has by no means restricted its grants to London ventures, and its example has influenced not a few civic authorities into following the national lead.

Obviously, then, the general theatrical picture has been utterly changed during the past few years. In earlier times those interested in dramatic experiments had been forced to rely largely upon the co-operation of amateur associations and play-producing clubs. Societies and clubs, of course, are still active, and their contributions have been increased by an upsurging of theatrical activities in the universities, but no longer are they the only, or the chief, supplements to the commercial stages.

It need hardly be said that thus a whole new world has opened out for young dramatists. Commercial managements, having no subsidies or guarantees, are compelled to play safe; they cannot afford to produce plays which, however promising, appear not likely to bring reasonably full houses; experimental novelties may appeal to them, but if the experimental forms are lacking in finish they are bound to reject them. There is nothing wrong with this, but of course it means that young writers with new ideas and new techniques may find it difficult to find opportunities for trying out their works before an audience. Now, with the recently established pattern of patronage at work, today's experimenters, thus supported by the Establishment, are being given ample scope for their activities.

The encouragement given to young writers, however, has not been the only contribution made by the non-commercial play-houses; they have also brought to notice scores of dramas from abroad. It is true that from 1900 onward English playgoers had had many opportunities of seeing new works by Continental and American authors; it is also true that some of these, such as the writings of Eugene O'Neill, Luigi Pirandello, and Karel Čapek, were of a then experimental kind; but for the most part the more extreme and bizarre experiments were neglected, and many of the productions could be seen only by a restricted number of spectators. As a symbol of this may be taken the fact that Alfred Jarry's *Ubu Roi*, although frequently alluded to in critical writings on the drama since its *première* in 1896, did not appear in an English version until 1966. Nowadays English audiences have the chance of seeing all kinds of foreign dramas, from older works to the very latest. In a short survey such as the present, of course, no space can be devoted to plays other than those by English authors: even the widely in-fluential *Waiting for Godot* must be omitted, since it was at the start composed in French (as *En attendant Godot*) by an Irish dramatist. Nevertheless, it must be borne in mind that, in the midst of the conditions operative today, numerous non-English plays are currently being accepted in our theatres as though they were native products and that consequently an understanding of recent dramatic work in England can hardly be attained without an appreciation of what has been happen-ing abroad.

This becomes particularly important when consideration is given to the medley of slogans and critical labels which now abound in such profusion. Many of these were known, in spirit if not always in name, to experimenters in the earlier years of the century. Thus, for example, the Theatre of Cruelty seems a novel innovation until we cast our thoughts back to the Grand Guignol seasons organized between 1920 and 1922 at the Little Theatre by José G. Levy, when Dame Sybil Thorndike and Sir Lewis Casson made notable appearances in macabre dramas and when skilfully executed posters showed chalk-faced spectators in the dress circle either wiping beads of perspiration from their brows or else slumped down in a faint; the concept of the Theatre of the Absurd has a long lineage; even 'anti-theatre' was spoken of, and there were some enthusiasts who went still further into the region of 'anti-actor' philosophy. At the same time these slogans and cults have much more force today, both because they have been augmented and intensified by increased knowledge of what is being done abroad and because what was merely talked about in the past is now being seen on the stage.

In themselves, it would seem, the slogans and the labels are being cultivated rather by directors than by playwrights, and therefore their main force has been productional rather than authorial; yet it must be admitted that the continual talk about these terms and their associated philosophies has to be taken into account when consideration is given to the problems confronting contemporary dramatists and to their individual lines of development. Indeed, this consideration leads us into the very core of the New Wave movement.

Although this New Wave must be regarded as part of a general dramatic development which finds its beginnings at the close of the nineteenth century, no one can deny that it was a revolution both in form and content. What went immediately before was, therefore, cast aside. Despite the numerous divergencies in the styles adopted by individual playwrights, divergencies which occasionally took shape as complete variations, a general architectural design prevailed during the period from 1930 to 1955. Whether a drama was realistically conceived or poetic in concept, its axial quality remained the same: it presented a story and it dealt with characters; its conventions were more or less stable.

In so far as form was concerned, the revolution tended to overthrow, or at the very least to question, all preceding assumptions. Plots might be dispensed with, and there might even be a denial that such a thing as 'character' can exist; the older conventions were regarded as old-fashioned and inappropriate for new situations and ideas. Thus, in approaching the New Wave drama, the first, and perhaps the most important, thing to be observed is that the playwrights have been forced to invent conventions of their own. This process of search for appropriate form and technique has necessarily involved the expenditure of considerable effort on the part of individual authors : frequently conventions, once found, have had to be laid aside in favour of others; sometimes one set of conventions which has been discovered, through practice, to prove not thoroughly satisfactory has been intermingled with conventions of a different kind; and, even when an author has finally found methods likely to permit him to express his own inner visions in fittingly dramatic terms, these methods are rarely suited for exploitation by his fellows. The young drama-tists of the past ten years have thus found themselves in a posi-tion wholly different from that of their predecessors. This con-trast between past and present can readily be illustrated by one single fact: during the earlier decades of the century appeared at least a dozen books on 'How to Write a Play'; some of them, like St John Ervine's, were written by distinguished dramatists or critics; they were bought and read by those who aspired to apply themselves to the theatre, and, although naturally play-writing cannot be taught, they were of service because a certain basic form was generally accepted. Today the preparation of any such guides would be absolutely unthinkable.

If the revolution reacted against previously established dramatic patterns it also rejected, in a very emphatic manner, much of the play content which had been current and familiar; and here, too, the new movement exhibits strange complexities.

One trend has been away from the 'drawing-room' towards the 'kitchen', from the comfortable middle-class environment towards those environments which had appealed to the repertory playwrights during the century's earlier decades. Nevertheless, even although this seems to be taking up where St John Ervine, Harold Brighouse, and others had left off, the atmosphere clearly is of an entirely different kind – an atmosphere not con-fined to the theatre but enveloping a great deal of popular literature, film, and television. In many of the repertory plays violent scenes had been presented, but in general the violence was presented as the result of known causes, and implicitly, if not explicitly, there was the assumption that all would be well if these causes were eradicated. Now, on the contrary, the vio-lence assumes another form: its sources are not patently evident; it appears to be pervasive everywhere; and, instead of being something deplorable, it has come to exercise a peculiar fascination. There is another difference as well. Whereas in former years violence had been associated with forces such as the conflict between Irish Catholicism and Protestantism, or between factory owners and their men, it now is intimately related to man's sexual instincts. It would, of course, be absurd to suggest that the popularity of the James Bond stories and of films modelled upon them derives from any inner philosophy; yet in these and kindred works we can readily sense the crude exhibition of prevailing moods. A vague sense of menace, often associated with claustrophobic fears; a sensation of loneliness, or perhaps one might say a sensation of being lost; a craving, frequently not acknowledged, for love and friendship, unsatisfied because of a dimly realized inadequacy in the heart; an emphasis upon sex, combining violent attraction with equally violent revulsion and sometimes moving from the heterosexual into other spheres; and, above all, ruthlessness – these qualities are so commonplace as to require no extended exposition.

The gradual spread of this atmosphere in novels, stories, and films has coincided with a new freedom within the theatre. There are few things nowadays which the Lord Chamberlain's office is willing to delete; and accordingly for playwrights the stage has presented even more exciting possibilities than have been felt by novelists or screen-play authors. A novelist in the past (and even, very occasionally, in the present) might be confronted by legal action, but in general he was, and still is, accorded far greater liberty than a dramatist, precisely because what is read differs from what is seen; and, although films were controlled, the issuing of variant licensing forms permitted considerable latitude. It is, therefore, perfectly understandable that in this new-found freedom, and with the pressure of popular literature around them, the dramatists eagerly applied themselves to fresh subject-matter.

They have done so, obviously, in many varied ways. Some of them, it would seem, have not gone very far beyond what might be called simple exploitation of scenes which, because of their stage novelty, were likely to startle and shock their audiences. On the other hand most of the young playwrights who have been active during the past decade clearly are animated by a deep sense of purpose and, in particular, by a mood of baffled anger. This mood has led them in various directions. It has encouraged satire directed at objects and persons which, to them, appear iniquitous and unjust and stupid; and it has also encouraged the development of the style to which has been given the name of 'sick humour'. While, however, the mood of baffled anger may at times be satisfactorily expressed in these ways, for other authors neither satire nor sick humour is enough. Some are so racked and despairing that they are impelled to go back to the tortured universe which writhes in the novels of Genet; for others the violence, the preoccupation with sex, the rebellious individualism may be so potent and confused that they cannot inhabit the range of the actual but take shape as dire phantasms and terrible nightmares.

Necessarily, therefore, the plays produced amid these conditions, even although there has been a general tendency to exploit certain common new-found material, have displayed a bewildering diversity both in technique and in purpose. In 1959 Shelah Delaney chose as her characters a girl made pregnant by a Negro, a prostitute of a mother, and a devotedly attendant homosexual; impotence and homosexuality go together in Bill Naughton's *All in Good Time* (1963) and promiscuity is the theme of his *Alfie* (1963): Lesbianism finds an exposition in Frank Marcus' *The Killing of Sister George* (1965): Nina Warner Hooke's *The Striplings* (1963) has been described as lust in a stable: in *Ride a Cock Horse* (1965) David Mercer makes a husband, his wife, and two mistresses twist themselves into queer parody cartoons of themselves, the man eventually huddling into the shape of a foetus: David Turner's *The Antique Shop* (1963) gives his hero three mistresses and a woman partner. In *Entertaining Mr Sloane* (1964) Joe Orton shows a youth who comes to a house seeking a bed-sitting-room; the brother and the sister who own the place both find him sexually attractive; he bashes in their father's head, but, instead of summoning the police, they decide to conceal the murder so that they can blackmail him into sharing his favours with them – six months for the brother, six months for the sister. Orton's later play, *Loot* (1966), becomes another prime piece for 'connoisseurs of outrage', with a central character in a young bank-robber who conceals his booty in his mother's coffin and who

K

gains macabre laughs while, in talking about "Spanish whores", he makes her false teeth click in fandango style. Charles Dyer's *Staircase* (1966) is a menacing study of a homosexual 'marriage'. Giles Cooper's *Everything in the Garden* (1962) sardonically exhibits outwardly respectable households turned into brothels – the husbands willingly, even anxiously, encouraging their wives – with murder thrown in. Murder, cruelty, and violence often take centre stage, as in David Rudkin's *Afore Night Come* (1962), dredging up from man's depths an irrational bestiality. Sometimes these forces are dealt with in a melodramatic and even in a melodramatically farcical manner; sometimes, invested with much symbolism, they are intermingled with visions of universal absurdity illustrating what is being called the 'human predicament'. Henry Livings produces *Kelly's Eye* (1963) alongside the satirical bitterness of *Stop It, Whoever You Are* (1961) and the bustling extravagance of *Eh?* (1964); a few years before, purposeful impossibilities were combined with exaggerated comedy in the fantastic world of N. F. Simpson's *A Resounding Tinkle* (1957) and *One Way Pendulum* (1959); and about the same time Spike Milligan and John Antrobus made the extravagance darker and more threatening, during the imagined aftermath of a Third World War, in *The Bed-sitting Room* (1963).

Within the universe fashioned by these and other experimental dramatists, perplexing in their variety, some four or five authors stand out, partly because the range of their plays is wide and partly because of the strong individual quality inherent in their writings; and to these obviously special attention must be given. And it is only right to start with John Osborne.

In 1956, as everyone knows, *Look Back in Anger* was accorded a rapturous reception at the Royal Court Theatre. In its planning this play offers little of novelty; basically it belongs to the realistic tradition and, although it ends with uncertainty rather than with a bold theatrical climax, it is in essence a story-drama. What gives it distinction is the powerful surge of Jimmy Porter's vituperation, a spate of words which mark its author as a master of prose. Since then Osborne has pursued an erratic and at times a bewildering track. *The Entertainer* (1957), which may well be considered his highest dramatic achievement, seemed to demonstrate his ability to move in more than a single narrow area and to reach beyond a subjective approach; but *Epitaph for George Dillon* (1957), written in collaboration with Anthony Creighton, brings us back to vituperation – and this vituperation rises to a self-defeating crescendo in *The World of Paul Slickey* (1959). The historical setting of *Luther*, produced a year or two later, suggested that once again he was moving forward, yet closer examination shows that this is not really an historical play: the deeper issues which instigated the Reformation have been ignored, and Luther himself is presented in such a manner as inevitably to recall the figure of Jimmy Porter. A step in a different direction was taken in *Inadmissible Evidence* (1964), wherein loneliness, a sense of inadequacy, and a suspicion of inner corruption are threateningly evoked within the terrible courtroom of a man's mind. One of the episodes in this drama sympathetically introduces a homosexual, and homosexuality completely invades the whole of *A Patriot for Me* (1965) – a puzzling work, not because its action lacks clarity or because its dialogue is obscure, but simply because of the difficulty in fathoming what basic purpose its author had in fashioning its scenes: maybe the thought of creating the shock of the homosexual ball fascinated him; maybe he saw the homosexuals as rebels persecuted by an unjust society – no one can tell. Similar puzzlement has been expressed concerning *A Bond Honoured* (1966), a one-act drama adapted from an early play by Lope de Vega, which has been described as an "excellent pre-Freudian case study of incest, sadism, masochism, and other sexual aberrations". Some have seen here a terrifying picture of the penalty which, all too soon, we shall have to suffer for the excesses of our present-day society; for others Osborne's purpose is to set up a figure whose will-power, inflexibility, and daring make him a hero to be admired. The only certainties are that even those many who have condemned the piece admit its theatrical forcefulness and that the author himself has adopted the somewhat extraordinary course of issuing an open declaration of "open and frontal war" – whatever that may mean – against "the puny theatre critics" who have dared to deal with his work adversely.

If we take these plays together there can be no doubt in our minds that Osborne has a vigorous, although often a somewhat over-emphatic command of dramatic language, especially in the magnificent rhetoric which wells up in his scenes of anger; yet here, in this very strength, one perhaps senses his chief limitation. A playwright usually finds his true scope in his adaptability, in his power to submerge himself in different characters. In such a play as *The Entertainer* Osborne seemed to be moving towards the attainment of that power, but in his other works he gives us the impression that he rarely can escape from himself and his surrounding circumstances.

In this he does not stand alone; many examples of similar concentration upon the author's self are to be found manifested diversely on today's stage. After Osborne, for instance, we are apt to think of Harold Pinter: the two writers at first would appear to dwell at opposing poles, the one fervid, dominated by emotion, apt to explode in passion at any moment, the other outwardly cool, almost clinical, inclined to allusiveness rather than bold statement: nevertheless, they are alike in presenting, each in his own peculiar manner, their own personal dreams and fears. *The Birthday Party* in 1958 first brought Pinter to critical attention, and since then both his stage-plays and his television dramas have introduced him to a wide public: *The Dumb Waiter*, *The Room*, and *The Caretaker* in 1960, *The Lover* and *The Dwarfs* in 1963, and *The Homecoming* in 1965. Stylistically these are all of a piece, with the employment of dialogue almost as far removed from Osborne's as could possibly be imagined: there is no rhetoric here, but sentences short, taut, and pointed, dictated by a cold, sardonic awareness of the absurdities of common speech. In action, too, there tends to be a suppression of movement, often confined within a closely cabined area, a setting which, taken in conjunction with the elusive dialogue, helps him to create a feeling of vague menace. Beyond these qualities, however, we find ourselves confronted by a puzzle. Unquestionably behind and beyond such plays as *The Birthday Party*, *The Dumb Waiter*, *The Room,* and *The Caretaker* symbols lurk in the gloom, but precisely what these symbols are and whether they all spring from the same source remains uncertain. There is at least a strong possibility that they are an amalgam of diverse elements, and that a similar diversity in dramatic motivation must be allowed for as we pass from

play to play. *The Dwarfs*, based on an apprentice novel, appears
to deal with boyhood fantasies, and any bafflement we experience is due to the 'private' nature of the action and the
fictionally conceived characters; in *The Caretaker* we possibly
may be in the presence of similar private symbols intertwined
with others of a wider significance; and, when we come to *The
Lover*, we must be prepared to make allowance for a deliberately conscious process of playmaking, where expertly planned
structure and calculated devices are designed primarily to arrest
audience attention. If this is so, then the peculiar feeling we
experience of alternately coming close to an understanding of
Pinter's objectives and of becoming utterly lost here finds its
explanation.

While there can be no hesitation in saying that Pinter is an
adroit expert in the handling of a particular kind of play, and
that the atmosphere he creates is largely dependent upon his
mastery of a very effective, although 'special', kind of theatrical
dialogue, certain qualifications are necessary. Every dramatist,
of course, has his own speech-forms: Shakespeare, Congreve,
Sheridan, Wilde, Shaw, all have individual voices of their own.
At the same time a dramatist ideally should have the ability
of adjusting his own voice, like a ventriloquist, to the characters
whom he sets on the stage. Pinter's dialogue is obviously distinctive, not because he invented its forms but because he has taken
a pattern and made it his own. Anyone who has seen Alfred
Hitchcock's film of 1938, *The Lady Vanishes*, will immediately
recognize in the dialogue of the two English cricket fans a style
of speech which is patently 'Pinter', and a similar technique can
readily be traced sporadically in other early cinematic and stage-
plays. In these, however, it had been restricted to short scenes
and to selected characters. What Pinter has done is to make it
universal, so that his characters are seldom marked off from
each other by what they say or by their way of saying it. Thus,
for example, we hear an old man, Max, talking in *The
Homecoming*:

> As soon as you stop paying your way here, I mean when
> you're too old to pay your way, you know what I'm going
> to do? I'm going to give you the boot. . . .
> Sure. I mean, bring in the money and I'll put up with you.
> But when the firm gets rid of you – you can flake off . . .

> One lot after the other. One mess after the other . . .
> Look what I'm lumbered with. One cast-iron bunch of crap
> after another. One flow of stinking pus after another.

A few moments later another and an entirely different person
is talking:

> What do you think of the room? Big, isn't it? It's a big house.
> I mean, it's a fine room, don't you think? . . .
> You'll be perfectly all right up there without me. Really you
> will. I mean, I won't be long. Look, it's just up there. It's
> the first door on the landing. The bathroom's right next
> door . . .
> You don't have to go to bed. I'm not saying you have to. I
> mean, you can stay up with me.

It need hardly be said that Pinter's dialogue holds an audience
and that many people do use language in this way: but not all
people use it in the same way, and the application of a set pattern to many different characters has the result of blurring the
distinctions between them. A somewhat kindred repetitive effect
is to be observed in his stage-directions. In general these directions are, like the dialogue itself, sparse and sparing: there
are no lengthy descriptions and explanations such as are
familiar in the writings of G.B.S. and his companions. The
cast-list of *The Homecoming* gives merely the names and ages
of the persons – "MAX, a man of seventy . . . LENNY, a man in
his early thirties . . . SAM, a man of sixty-three" – nothing
about who or what they are: so stinted, indeed, are the comments that one is surprised to note that the author wastes even
a few words in telling us that Max, Lenny, and Sam is each "a
man" and that Ruth is "a woman". The specification of the
setting is equally economic, even to the use of technical abbre-
viations – R., L., and U.L. – of a sort once familiar in early
French's play-texts; so, too, the indications of action are kept
down to a minimum. In the midst of all this one repeated stage-
direction – "Pause" – attracts attention: within the course of
The Homecoming it appears, occasionally half a dozen times
on a single page, more than 220 times; and the multiplication of
the pauses cannot be explained by the author's desire to have
distinctions made between episodes requiring rapid movement
and others demanding an *adagio* effect: they are spread evenly
throughout the entire play. Usually a skilled playwright seeks

by the manipulation of his dialogue to tell his actors when the
tempo should be changed, when rests are called for, and when
silence should become pregnant with meaning; and it is rather
hard to explain why Pinter, admittedly adept, has felt it necessary to repeat himself in this way. Might it be suggested that
the device is employed precisely because there is so little variation in the speech patterns?

Perhaps these 'pauses' may be associated with another
peculiarity in Pinter's plays. There can be not the slightest doubt
but that he has a sensitively keen and subtle ear for language
apt to come easily from actors' lips: because of this his dialogue
has been eagerly praised by those who have to interpret his
words on the stage and it has charmed those listening to it. On
the other hand it may be wondered whether he, himself an
actor, has not been inclined to leave too much to the performers
by providing silences, both short and long, in central scenes.
In *The Homecoming*, for example, the actress who takes the
part of Ruth can, through gesture and demeanour, give the
spectators a foretaste of what she is revealed to be towards the
end of the play; but if we confine our attention to the dialogue,
there is absolutely nothing to indicate that Teddy and Ruth
are not what they seem to be – a respectable married couple,
with three young children, she tired after a journey and thinking of those children who may be missing her and he, even in
the midst of his excitement at returning to his old home, solici-
tous for her. The result of this is that, unless the actress playing
Ruth inserts what is not in the text, the whole climax of the
piece becomes almost incomprehensible: and even when produced precisely as the author wished, we seem to be confronted
by a clash between what is designed as pregnant silence and
what has been designed in terms of the surprise technique. Not
without justification an amusing article by Michael Frayne
draws attention to this. The article is entitled "£earn-to-Rite
Black Comedy":

> Someone starts making love to a woman whose husband is
> present. How does the husband react? Does he hit the in-
> truder, become embarrassed, storm out of the room? All
> these reactions are tired and obvious. We want something
> brand-new, the £EARN-TO-RITE Special – NO REAC-
> TION!

Let's take it further. The wife (mother of three; husband a university professor) is invited by her father-in-law and two brothers-in-law to set up as their joint mistress, and to keep them all by becoming a prostitute. Gasp, gasp – titter, titter. But wait! How does she respond? With horror? Embarrassment? Prurient curiosity? Not if she's done the £EARN-TO-RITE Black Comedy Course! She responds with NOTHING, apart from insisting that as a prostitute she'll need a flat with at least three rooms!

This mocking fiction may seem exaggerated, but the fiction, of course, is founded on fact; and there is at least the possibility that Michael Frayne is critically nearer the mark than those who speak in hushed wonderment about *The Homecoming*'s deep symbolism and mythical quality.

Arnold Wesker inhabits an entirely different world, where an attempt is made to render everything crystal clear. Like Osborne and Pinter, however, he also is self-centred, and his plays might be described as essentially autobiographical, always reflecting his own personal experiences: yet between them and him there exists a wide gulf. Osborne rises to his fullest dramatic height when he finds or devises an opportunity for the expression of anger. Pinter sometimes seems to go back to boyhood nightmares, sometimes he looks upon the aberrations of humanity with a cold and contemptuous eye. Wesker, in spite of the autobiographical quality of his writings, has a wide interest in his fellow-beings and in the betterment of their conditions; he is a rather naïve rebel, often puzzled and occasionally despondent, but always intent upon action. Instead of moving from boyhood nightmares to a strange half-real, half-stylized world, he starts from a boyhood reality and directs his gaze towards dreams for the future. His practical endeavours to stimulate working-class interest in the theatre should, therefore, be seen as a basic counterpart of his work as a dramatist. He could no more have conceived the menacing barrenness of *The Caretaker*'s grim walls and its three tortured characters than Pinter could have conceived *The Kitchen* (1959) filled with its pots and pans, peopled by a crowd of Italians and Frenchmen, Germans and Irish, Jamaicans, Cypriots, and Cockneys. At the same time *The Kitchen* in a sense has its own claustrophobic atmosphere, and it, too, has its symbolic overtones, although overtones openly expressed and lacking Pinter's elusiveness. As a craftsman Pinter is subtle, often so subtle as to remain bafflingly obscure, whereas Wesker's strength flows from his frank, open, and lively interest in the world around him: the menacing mood of *The Dumb Waiter* arises from the feeling that the characters are shut up within a confined space which is strange to them; the confined space of *The Kitchen* is all too real and familiar. The famous Wesker Trilogy (1958–60) owes its appeal to the great flowing sweep of its action and to its rich range of character delineation, perhaps lacking in subtlety, but intensely and warmly conceived. Unfortunately, however, even in his best plays, *Chips with Everything* (1962) and the component parts of the Trilogy, Wesker fails to make full theatrical impact because of a certain simpleness both in attitude and in composition. As his latest drama, *Their Very Own and Golden City* (written 1964:1966), clearly demonstrates, honesty of purpose, compassion, and the sincere desire to improve existing social conditions are not sufficient in themselves to make a great play.

All these three authors take their places within the scope of the realistic tradition, each adapting it to suit his own ends: Wesker remains closest to the relatively straightforward reproduction of ordinary speech, Osborne enriches it with rhetoric, Pinter evolves out of common conversation a sardonically conceived pattern of dialogue. In following this tradition, of course, they are consistently and logically pursuing the course established in the first flush of enthusiasm during the mid-fifties, when the poetic styles of Eliot and Fry were rejected. Elsewhere, however, it is not difficult to trace signs of uneasiness among the new wave of playwrights. Even Wesker, the most realistically inclined of them all, has admitted recently that "realistic art is a contradiction in terms". Numbers among their companions have been striving, in various ways, to seek out means whereby their dramatic scenes might be made more colourful and raised beyond the level of the particular and the commonplace.

Even before the formal advent of the new movement John Whiting had sought to achieve this end chiefly through the use of symbols. *A Penny for a Song* was a remarkable play for the year 1951, although the problems and dangers inherent in his approach were demonstrated almost at the same time in *Saint's Day*: writing of this second piece, the author expressed the opinion that in fact his symbols were "simple"; no doubt they were so for him, but both in the original production and in revival they tended to leave audiences in a state of baffled irritation. *Marching Song* in 1954 came closer towards reaching satisfactory artistic form, but even it and its successor *The Devils* (1961), although skilfully and imaginatively wrought, somehow failed to justify the hopes which so many had had in his talent. Unfortunately Bernard Kops, after his attractively original experiments in *The Hamlet of Stepney Green* (1958) and *The Dream of Peter Mann* (1960), has become silent, and several others have fallen by the wayside. Among them, however, stands out one writer who in many respects might be regarded as the most interesting of our present-day dramatists.

Concerning the quality inherent in the works of John Arden certainly difference of opinion, even controversy, reigns; and the conflicting attitudes depend both upon the unevenness in his own writing and, still more, on the originality of his approach to theme and form. In the introductory note to the printed text of *Live Like Pigs* (produced in 1958) he states clearly, first, that in writing this piece he was more concerned with the 'poetic' than with the 'journalistic' and that his presentation of the respectable Jacksons and the disreputable Sawneys was not dictated by any doctrinaire attitude: like a true dramatist, he sought to understand his characters – both groups, he said, "uphold standards of conduct that are incompatible, but which are both valid in their correct context". With this note we may take another – that which is attached to the text of *The Waters of Babylon* (produced in 1957): this play deals with a sordid problem – rack-renting and municipal corruption – and one might have supposed that the author would have wished its setting to be thoroughly realistic; instead, he declares that

> the sort of scenery I had in mind was the eighteenth or early nineteenth century sort, which involved the use of sliding flats or drop curtains which open and close while the actors are still on stage – a method still in use in provincial pantomimes.

These two notes serve as clues to his fundamental approach, and they agree with his constant attempt to secure stylistic variety and expansion through the introduction of songs in the midst of his realistic dialogue, or else through a sudden movement from 'ordinary' speech to poetic expression. In *The Waters of Babylon,* for example, Krank is talking to Barbara: "What has there been between you and that girl?" she asks in a strained voice; "Nothing, dear Miss Baulkfast," he replies, "that need cause you to lose your sleep"; she repeats the question in a slightly different form, "What has there been between you and *this* girl?" and he starts to reply, "Nothing, dear Miss Baulkfast, that . . ." Then suddenly he turns on her:

Now listen to me: To look for true love in a naked bed
It is more dangerous, perhaps more vain,
Than burgling a house on fire,
Pearl diving under a whirling roof of sharks,
Hewing pit coal when the narrow air hangs dead along the
    galleries.
Where is your gain?
You do not have to do it for a living.
You do not have to fight it as a war:
You look for too much, and you look too far.
That way you find nothing but another person's pain.
And then you delude yourself, it's a fit pain for *you* to bear:
Though all you know about it is a muttering you would hear
Drift into your ears when you think you're asleep in bed.
Alone in bed, I mean: *I* never talk in my sleep.
It looks like I've lost a page from the Specification of the
    Hampstead school. Do you know where it might be?

And so we return to prose. That Arden, perhaps more than any other contemporary playwright, has been tortured by his search for conventions and forms fitted to his needs probably explains the peculiar diversity and disparate qualities of his writings. In *Serjeant Musgrave's Dance* (1959) he produces something of assured strength; his unhappy experiment in *The Happy Haven,* with its rather weak allegory buttressed by the employment of masks, seems a sad descent, and *The Workhouse Donkey* (1963), despite its liveliness, leaves us dissatisfied unless we assume – what is by no means certain – that here he was going to an extreme in planning his comedy in such a manner as to allow the spectators absolutely complete freedom to make up their minds about the characters and the events. From hilarious comedy with a bitter tang he next turns back in a fresh direction towards the ballads, presenting in *Armstrong's Last Good-Night* (1964) a grim story of a barbaric Border hero in his clash with a politer, more civilized, and more intellectually acute environment; this is followed by a second historical drama, *Left-handed Liberty* (1965), a study of King John and the framing of Magna Carta which, although occasionally it allows its characters to slip into a meshing net of ideas, amply reveals the liveliness of his mind and his theatrical skill; and, as has already been noted, that play has a successor in an entirely different style – *The Royal Pardon* (1966), ostensibly a children's piece, but with an appeal to more than the very young. Suppleness, vigour, and strength Arden manifestly possesses, and, despite the fact that his achievements to date have been unequal, it seems certain that in the future those who will look back upon our stage will single him out for special attention.

What has been accomplished during these ten years is assuredly remarkable. No one would deny that some of the *avant-garde* plays are imitative rather than creative in form and that in some the themes have been chosen shallowly instead of being wrought out of deep conviction; but could we have expected otherwise? Has there been any period in the theatre's history when the lesser did not co-exist with the greater? What is certain is that in their larger and more significant efforts the New Wave dramatists have opened up fresh vistas and explored territory hitherto almost, if not entirely, neglected. Nevertheless, if we want fully to appreciate what they have done and if we wish to distinguish between what may prove to be passing fashions and what appears to be creatively valuable, we must go just a little further.

14

The Modern Drama :

A FIFTH MOVEMENT

"I DON'T want to exaggerate this famous revolution that everybody talks about."

That statement was made, in 1964, by a man active in the theatre and almost universally known. He went on to suggest that at the moment we are "in a period of hiatus" and that "after all, there's no reason why an effusion like the one of 1956 should appear more than once every ten years." Still further he proceeded, claiming that the division "between the West End and the opposition theatre" was becoming blurred and that the initial impetus of the latter was already showing signs of losing its force. Many of the earlier writers, he thought,

simply wrote themselves out: they became famous so quickly that they lost the impulse to break through the barrier of public indifference. And now smart magazines will print anything they care to send in. It's too easy . . . Nowadays everybody wants to be 'with it'; there must be a place for people who don't want to be with it, because they are the people who create the with-its.

Reading these remarks, we might readily assume that they had been uttered by a spokesman of the West End, and because of that assumption we might be prepared to dismiss them in a summary and contemptuous manner.

But who, in fact, was speaking?

These words came from the wisest and most stimulating leader of the new wave of young playwrights, from the creator and inspirer of the English Stage Company, from George Devine. Obviously they demand careful examination; obviously, too, they call for an attempt to look around us, keeping in mind our knowledge of the general progress of the English theatre, in an attempt to estimate where we stand. Implied in Devine's comments is the thought of both past and future: we know, of course, that most speculations concerning the way in which our contemporary dramatic activities will be regarded half a century from now must necessarily be uncertain, if not completely vain, that the patterns of the past need not be repeated, and that what's to come is still unsure. Yet these reflections of George Devine do give justification for at least a hesitant and tentative inquiry; indeed, it might be said that they make such an inquiry imperative.

Of one thing we may be reasonably certain: in after-times theatrical historians will find the new wave revolution the most characteristic development in the fourth movement of the modern theatre, and they will discover that the nearest parallel to the present decade is the decade between 1600 and 1610. In relating these two periods they will note many likenesses: some of these have already been briefly discussed, but here they call for further emphasis. The 'private' playhouses which flourished during the first years of the seventeenth century were those which mainly encouraged the young rebels of that age: although they were not subsidized, they did stand apart from what might be regarded as the Elizabethan-Jacobean 'West End' – the great public theatres, of which the Globe was the mighty symbol. In the dramas produced during the two periods the likenesses embrace both elements of strength and elements of weakness. The serious intensity inspiring the playwrights created

then, and recently has created, an awareness of new theatrical
potentialities expressing itself alike in choice of subject-matter,
basic treatment of the selected themes, and technical methods.
At the same time it is impossible to avoid noticing that the intensity itself leads towards, and perhaps cannot be dissociated
from, an implication of moral superiority. During Jacobean
times Ben Jonson was by no means alone in ridiculing popular
dramatic styles and in proclaiming his own rectitude; and a
similar attitude has been spread through many modern productions. And this rectitude has not always resulted in theatrical
power and success: despite Jonson's manifest admiration for
Shakespeare, he ridiculed several lines in *Julius Caesar* and
presumably wrote his own *Catiline* and *Sejanus* to show how
classical subjects ought to be dealt with; but whereas *Julius
Caesar* remains vital, the other two dramas have long been
dead.

In looking dispassionately at the manifestations of the revolutionary mood in the earlier plays, we must, moreover,
acknowledge that frequently it was connected with concepts
narrow and one-sided, the consequence either of a desperate
desire to seem original or of a failure to see things in the round.
Jonson's companion, George Chapman, illustrates this well.
That he was a writer of considerable merit is certain, yet in his
poems and in his plays we constantly stumble upon absurdities:
sometimes these arise from his desire to be 'different', conducing
to his love of the paradoxical, as when he makes one of his
heroes enter into a lengthy argument in defence of the terrible
Massacre of St Bartholomew; sometimes the absurdities come
from the fact that, in his self-centred intensity, he has not
thought out his ideas carefully enough. Similar ideas and judg-
ments are not lacking in contemporary works. One example will
serve for many. In 1965 the English Stage Company produced
Edward Bond's *Saved* at the Royal Court: this showed a baby
stoned to death in a London park. To his printed text of the play
the author has added a preface in which he stresses that this
scene of brutality is as nothing when put alongside other greater
real-life brutalities of our time. This statement is obviously
true, and to most of us surely will come the thought of the cold-
blooded, malevolent slaughter of thousands upon thousands of
children in German concentration camps. But all Bond can say

is that "compared to the 'strategic' bombing of German towns" his own fictional episode "is a negligible atrocity". The parallel with Chapman seems complete.

The same intensity, too, led and leads towards such a concentration upon indignant resentment as can leave no room for other emotions. Already it has been suggested that, although Jonson's *Volpone* is a great literary work, as a play it defeats its own ends and becomes theatrically dulled by its single-minded destructive effort to present mankind in terms of beasts and birds of prey, with practically no alleviating contrast. Among the dramas of our age there are obviously many conceived in the same way, sometimes directly following the Jonsonian approach by concentrating upon the terrors of bestiality, sometimes moving inversely by taking animalism as a virtue. A recent comment by Ronald Bryden on *Belcher's Luck* (1966) might justifiably be extended to several authors other than David Mercer: in Mercer's works Bryden remarks that there has always been something incomplete:

> They present heroes in wild, anarchic flight from modern life, who rail with comic violence against its empty, mechanical conformities, but never suggest how its hollowness might be filled. They simply retire to mental hospitals, arguing that the only sane adjustment to Western society is maladjustment, to dream of lost animal selves symbolized by sleek, pacific leopards or kindly gorillas.

The pacific leopards and the kindly gorillas may seem at first to inhabit a cage utterly different from that which holds Corbaccio and Voltore; but essentially these two cages were built on the same pattern.

If we are trying to assess the total dramatic accomplishments of the decade from 1600 to 1610 we realize, of course, that exclusive concentration upon the writings of Marston, Middleton, Jonson, and Chapman inevitably must give a distorted picture of the whole; not only would it leave out some of Shakespeare's most characteristic work, it would draw our attention away from several important trends within the theatre of that period. It is, therefore, certain that future historians will find themselves forced to consider more than what the New Wave authors have offered during the period between 1956

and 1966. Of course they will observe that no Shakespeare is to
be found, but it would have been foolish to expect anything of
the kind. Of course, too, they will dismiss almost all the
ephemeral farces, light comedies, musicals, and detective plays
just as we dismiss the majority of kindred pieces emanating
from earlier periods: here, perhaps, they will pause only long
enough to note the extraordinary breaking of previous records
by the sixteen-year run of Agatha Christie's *The Mousetrap*.
Yet, when they have winnowed away the lesser, they will not
fail to see that these ten years have not been without the presentation of numerous non-experimental dramas possessing
genuine value. They will probably draw attention to *The Long
Sunset* (1955), in which R. C. Sherriff, an author who won his
greatest success nearly thirty years ago with *Journey's End*,
thoughtfully, compassionately, and convincingly designed his
own picture of the human predicament. During the course of
the decade they will follow the career of Terence Rattigan,
whose *Ross* was one of the triumphs of the year 1960 and whose
Flare Path (1942), *The Winslow Boy* (1946), and *The Deep
Blue Sea* (1952) were among the more distinguished plays in
the period just before the new wave surged in. They will observe, too, that 1960 likewise witnessed the appearance of
Robert Bolt's *A Man for All Seasons* and *The Tiger and the
Horse*, works of prime worth penned by a young author who,
although he has affinities with contemporary theatrical rebels
and knows his Brecht as intimately as any of them, deliberately
declared that "simply to slap your audience in the face satisfies"
merely the "austere and puritanical streak" which runs in many
of Brecht's disciples, and is "a dangerous game to play" – and
who, in presenting his own 'Common Man', specifically de-
fined that character, not in restrictive proletarian terms, but as
one who expresses "what is common to all of us". They will
direct attention to the wide scope of Peter Shaffer's dramatic
work from the skilful and penetrating *Five Finger Exercise*
of 1958, through *The Private Ear* and *The Public Eye* of 1962,
to *The Royal Hunt of the Sun* in 1964, and *Black Comedy* in
1965. The interestingly 'Chekhovian' and perceptive *Lily in
Little India* (1965) by Donald Howarth is likely to be remembered, and there will be a record of how in 1963 and 1964
James Saunders, an individualistic 'outsider' (his own self-

L

description), stirred audiences with sensitively imaginative dialogue and evocative vision in *Next Time I'll Sing to You* and *A Scent of Flowers*. And, besides such plays, there will no doubt be others within this sphere considered to merit more notice than many 'experimental' efforts in the areas of "Happenings", of "The Theatre of Menace", and of what has been styled "The Theatre of Embarrassment."

Tentatively, then, we may reasonably suppose that some such picture of the playhouse of our time will be presented in the future, and the picture agrees in the main with George Devine's comments. But these comments, brief as they are, involve something more than merely a few passing reflections on actual achievements: they go further, suggesting that the time is approaching for the emergence of a still newer movement when possibly there might be a synthesis of the best in the two opposing styles.

Our initial reaction may well be to say that a development of this kind is most improbable : indeed, it would be perfectly easy to adduce arguments designed to demonstrate that the animosity and opposition between the two theatres is at present even fiercer than it ever has been. Yet, if we are prepared to look more closely, we cannot avoid noting at least some indications of change on the face of the theatrical barometer.

The first of these is the evident change within the commercial playhouses. Ordinary audiences attending their productions continue to ask that they should receive 'entertainment' for the money they hand over at the box-office for their seats, but, in addition to welcoming such serious plays as those of Robert Bolt, they are showing themselves prepared to accept dramatic works of a kind which certainly would not have been accepted ten years ago. Orton's *Entertaining Mr Sloane*, if it had been written in 1956, would most probably have been presented only at the Royal Court or at a theatre club : in 1964 it appeared at Wyndham's under the auspices of a commercial management.

Nor are there lacking corresponding signs within the other camp: George Devine's remarks about the new writers and the conditions surrounding them find reflection elsewhere. Ann Jellicoe, author of *The Sport of My Mad Mother* in 1956 and of *The Knack* in 1961, has lately stressed the disturbing effect resultant upon cultivation of the newest fads, an effort which, in her opinion, puts inescapable emphasis upon novelty of form leading to "a kind of desperate smartness". Another enthusiastic supporter of the experimental playwrights has been induced to confess that his objection to the 'well-made' style rests, not upon any objection to this dramatic pattern in itself, but simply upon the fact that it had commonly been employed to deal only with upper-class characters and situations. When *Saint's Day*, widely spoken of by experimental authors as a seminal drama, was revived in 1965, many of its proponents were disappointed and there was a feeling that, in the words of one critical spectator, it appeared to be in fact "rather a fusty and wizened play".

Perhaps the signs illustrated by these few examples may seem rather faint, even although we cannot deny that around us are to be discerned unmistakable indications of an alteration in established attitudes, together with occasional positive attempts, as in Alun Owen's *A Little Winter Love* (1963), to combine experimental form with older technique. And unquestionably we cannot escape a fundamental cleavage in approach towards the question of the theatre's function in its social environment. It may be profitable to exemplify the two contrasting attitudes by a couple of recent statements.

Martin Esslin, expert chronicler of the Theatre of the Absurd, declares that in essence this movement

> does not reflect despair or a return to dark irrational forces but expresses modern man's endeavour to come to terms with the world in which he lives. It attempts to make him face up to human condition as it really is, to free him from illusions that are bound to cause constant maladjustment and disappointment. There are enormous pressures in our world that seek to induce mankind to bear the loss of faith and moral certainties by being drugged into oblivion — by mass entertainments, shallow material satisfactions, pseudo-explanations of reality, and cheap ideologies. At the end of that road lies Huxley's Brave New World of senseless euphoric automata. Today, when death and old age are increasingly concealed behind euphemisms and comforting baby talk, and life is threatened with being smothered in the mass consumption of hypnotic mechanized vulgarity, the need to confront man with the reality of his situation is

greater than ever. For the dignity of man lies in his ability to face reality in all its senselessness; to accept it freely, without fear, without illusions – and to laugh at it. This is the cause to which, in their various individual, modest and quixotic ways, the dramatists of the Absurd are dedicated.

The assumption here is that it is the theatre's mission to teach and strengthen the spectators by a frank presentation of the violence, the brutalities, the enormities of present-day existence. Two years after the appearance of Esslin's words in 1962, Noël Coward composed a special introduction for a television version of his *Blithe Spirit*. "I knew in my teens," he said,

that the world was full of hatred, cruelty, vice, unrequited love, despair, destruction and murder. I also knew at the same time that it was filled with kindness, pleasure, joy, requited love, fun, excitement, generosity, laughter and friends. And through all my years I have never changed in my mind the balance of these absurd phenomena.

I do become increasingly exasperated, however, when in my own beloved profession everything that I have been brought up and trained to believe in is now decried. Nowadays a well-constructed play with a beginning, a middle and an end is despised, and a light comedy whose sole purpose is to amuse is dismissed as being trivial and insignificant. Since when has laughter been so insignificant?

The assumption in this statement is that the theatre's business is to entertain.

These two declarations appear to be in absolute opposition to each other, and yet we are bound to observe that they allude to the same things – cruelty, despair, absurdity, laughter: and this may persuade us to look at them more carefully. If we consider them separately as expositions of two contrasting schools of theatrical thought, then separate and incompatible they remain; but, if we put them together, we realize that, in spite of their antagonistic views, both are so measured and so broad in their conceptions as to seem not without the possibility of conjunction. Although Esslin does not refer specifically to entertainment, we sense that he is wise enough to make full allowance for the theatre's entertaining power; and, although Coward's final sentence alludes to light comedy, we know that the author of *The Vortex*, a play which made him in 1924 the leader of the youthful revolt which lies behind the revolt of to-day, would not confine entertainment to fleeting laughter alone. Coward would certainly include *King Lear* within his sphere, and Esslin would welcome its power not only to reveal life's darkness but also to entertain an audience.

So long as the opposing attitudes are of this kind, all is well: danger arises only when they become narrowly and crudely doctrinaire, so that one group refuses to see little or nothing that is entertaining save triviality and surface excitement, while the other becomes so intent upon confronting man with the reality of his situation that scenes of violence, in their mounting repetition, cease to make any deep impact. Clearly the one, in an extreme form, can end up by being merely an anodyne, reducing the word 'entertainment' until it applies only to what is sedative and vulgarly satisfying: the other, in its extreme form, can end up by defeating its own ends and by theatening the destruction of those peculiar qualities which give the theatre its distinction among the arts.

This leads to a final, and a fundamental, question.

In December 1966 there was a radio interview with the newly elected President of the Royal Academy, during which he declared his belief that painters, in the process of creating their works, have nothing to do with the public, that their sole concern is, or ought to be, with themselves. Whether or not that belief is shared by all those concerned with pictorial art does not matter for us: but with absolute certainty we can say that no similar statement could be made concerning the art theatrical. For everyone associated with the playhouse an audience is obligatory: indeed, as any knowledge of theatre history demonstrates, it is both formative and indirectly creative. Consequently we may be assured that whatever dramatic developments take shape in the immediate future will be largely determined by the nature of the public which the playhouses succeed in attracting during those years.

Theatre history suggests something else – that the theatres in the past which encouraged the greatest and longest-enduring dramas were those which, like Shakespeare's Globe, appealed to the most broadly representative body of spectators. Naturally, the true creative power rests in the shaping imaginative genius of the dramatist, but the full opportunity for the expressing of this genius and the stimulation of its widest potentialities seem to come when the practising playwright has the task of appealing to all kinds and manners of men.

Unfortunately such conditions as were operative in the Elizabethan period appear but seldom, and certainly the mid-years of the present century saw the range of regular theatre-goers declining and, more significantly, narrowing. Because of that, one of the most salutory endeavours of those associated with the New Wave has been their determined effort to arouse interest in the theatre among the youth of the community. This they have done, as we know, by concentrating upon productions rebellious, wrathful, satirical, shocking.

While the effort in itself is to be thoroughly applauded, there is a double danger – first, the danger that, in attracting one group by means of plays specially composed for their tastes, many members of the already existing theatre-going public may be estranged, and, secondly, that a kind of theatrical Hamlet-complex may come into being, with praise being given to certain dramas precisely because they are caviare to all save sectional groups. At the moment, then, we seem to be in a dilemma. On the one hand even a rapid glance at the list of "Long Runs on the London Stage" which is printed in *Who's Who in the Theatre* makes rather depressing reading: although this catalogue does include several plays of genuine worth, these are swamped by the titles of pieces trivial and jejune. On the other hand, before concentrating all our contempt upon the tastes which encourage these long runs, we may be wise to consider another of Noël Coward's reflections. He complains that the new theatre will often allow no alleviation for "the set grim patina of these dire years", and he adds

> We must all just sit and wait for death, or hurry it on according to how we feel. To my mind one of the most efficacious ways of hurrying it on is to sit in the theatre and look at a verbose, ill-constructed play acted with turgid intensity, which has received rave notices and is closing on Saturday.

One thing, however, deserves particular notice. Already

attention has been drawn to the validity of George Devine's observation concerning the changes within the two theatres, and these seem to be associated with an increasing awareness of the dilemma and with at least tentative moves being made towards its solution. If this is indeed a trend likely to be pursued further, then there may be reason for ending this survey by reverting to its start, with another reference to two plays, *The Thwarting of Baron Bolligrew* and *The Royal Pardon*. Of these, as we have seen, the latter has been described as born of the desire to find "some modern equivalent for the community drama of the Middle Ages"; Martin Browne, in discussing the former, notes how its humour and underlying seriousness have been made to appeal both to children and their parents; "these," he says, "are the audiences which the theatre has been in danger of losing, and an additional reason to salute this play is that it has brought them back".

APPENDIX

THE FEW SURVIVORS

Stage revivals from 1954 *to* 1965

[This list records revivals of English plays, from medieval times up to
1939, within the years 1954–65. Although an effort has been made to
render it as inclusive as possible, it makes no pretension to be a complete
catalogue of such productions: no doubt many other performances could
be added if an exhaustive survey were to be made of amateur dramatic
club activities. As it stands, however, it gives a reasonably accurate picture of the fate of the earlier drama in the modern period.

The plays of Shakespeare have been excluded since these obviously
stand apart and distinct from the others. Just how many thousands of
dramas have been contributed to the English theatre throughout the
course of more than five centuries cannot be estimated, nor has an
accurate count been made of the thousands which have come down to us
in printed texts: but obviously the few titles in the present list demonstrate the pitifully meagre number which survive on the stage—and this
number would become markedly more pitiful if attention were confined
solely to major professional productions. A considerable proportion of
the performances catalogued here were presented by amateurs, and
others, although professional, were confined to summer festival seasons.
In considering this list, on the other hand, it should be remembered, first,
that at least some dramatic works which no longer appear to be stageworthy have exerted an influence in printed form and, secondly, that
the selected period, 1954–65, does not include a few other dramas which,
in previous revivals, have captured the attention of the public. Thus, for
example, this period witnessed only two or three productions of Restoration comedies although these had flourished during the twenties and
the thirties.]

Fourteenth Century to 1580
The Mystery Cycles
[During recent years many medieval plays have been performed in
modernized, condensed versions. The most important are: *York* series,
originally prepared by J. S. Purvis for presentation at York in 1951,
repeated thereafter at the triennial Festival; *Chester* series, first given
in 1951, repeated in 1952, 1957, 1962, and 1967; *Wakefield* series, prepared in 1952 by Martial Rose, used in 1955 (Players of St Peter-upon-
Cornhill), 1961, and 1965 (at the Mermaid), and 1962 (by the Lambeth
Dramatic Club at Westminster Abbey); the so-called *'Ludus Coventriae'*,
now thought to belong to Lincoln, prepared by E. Martin Browne for
performance at the Coventry Festival in 1962, repeated there in 1964,
at Winchester Cathedral in 1965, and at Llandaff Cathedral in 1967;
a somewhat fuller version by Martial Rose appeared in Lincolnshire in
1966. In 1963 a 'composite cycle', made up of selected plays from

various sources by John Barton, was given by the Royal Shakespeare Company at St George's Church, Notting Hill. There have also been numerous performances of individual playlets in adapted forms.]

John Skelton
  Magnyfycence
    1963 : Tavistock Repertory.
Sir David Lindsay
  The Thrie Estaites
    1959 : Edinburgh Festival.
'Mr S.'
  Gammer Gurton's Needle
    1959 : Birmingham Repertory.
Nicholas Udall.
  Ralph Roister Doister
    1954 : Oxford University Players.

1580–1642
John Lyly
  Midas
    1959 : Hovenden Theatre Club.
Christopher Marlowe
  Tamburlaine
    1960 : Oxford University Dramatic Society.
    1964 : Tavistock Repertory.
  Edward II
    1954 : Oxford University Players at Edinburgh Festival.
    1956 : Stratford East.
           Ludlow Festival.
    1958 : Marlowe Society, Cambridge.
    1964 : Leicester Phoenix Theatre Company at New Arts.
  The Jew of Malta
    1954 : Marlowe Players of Reading University.
    1964 : Stratford-upon-Avon; 1965, Aldwych.
  Dr Faustus
    1956 : Tavistock Repertory.
    1960 : Marlowe Society, Cambridge.
    1961 : Old Vic.
  Dido
    1959 : Marlowe Society at Questors.
  The Massacre at Paris
    1963 : Marlowe Society, Cambridge.
Robert Greene
  James IV
    1958 : Drama Department of Bristol University.
  Friar Bacon
    1960 : Marlowe Society, Cambridge.

Henry Porter
The Two Angry Women of Abingdon
1956: Abingdon Drama Club.
(Unknown authors)
Arden of Feversham
1954: Stratford East.
1961: Arts, Cambridge.
1962: Theatre Royal, Margate; presented at the Lyric, Hammersmith, in 1963.
Fratricide Punished
1955: Questors.
1958: Birmingham Repertory.
A Yorkshire Tragedy
1958: Birmingham Repertory.
Thomas Dekker
The Shoemakers' Holiday
1954: Unity.
Bristol Old Vic.
1962: Old Vic.
1964: Mermaid.
Anthony Munday (and others)
Sir Thomas More
1954: Theatre Centre, London.
1964: Playhouse, Nottingham.
Ben Jonson
Every Man in his Humour
1960: Stratford East.
Volpone
1955: Stratford East.
Marlowe Society, Cambridge.
Bristol Old Vic.
The Alchemist
1957: Birmingham Repertory.
1962: Old Vic.
Keswick Festival.
1965: Meadow Players, at Playhouse, Oxford.
Epicœne
1965: Oxford University Dramatic Society.
Bartholomew Fair
1959: Oxford University Experimental Theatre Club.
George Chapman
Bussy D'Ambois
1954: Hovenden Theatre Club.
The Revenge of Bussy D'Ambois
1956: Hovenden Theatre Club.
Eastward Ho! (written with Jonson and Marston)
1962: Mermaid.

Thomas Middleton
  The Changeling
    1954: Pegasus Theatre Society at Wyndham's.
    1956: Oxford University Experimental Theatre Club.
    1961: Royal Court.
  A Chaste Maid in Cheapside
    1956: Leeds University Union Theatre Group.
    1961: Central School of Speech.
  Women Beware Women
    1962: Royal Shakespeare Theatre at Arts.
John Marston
  The Dutch Courtesan
    1954: Stratford East.
    1959: Stratford East.
    1964: National Theatre.
Cyril Tourneur
  The Revenger's Tragedy
    1954: Toynbee Hall.
      Oriel College Dramatic Society.
    1959: Marlowe Society, Cambridge.
    1965: Pitlochry Festival.
John Webster
  The Duchess of Malfi
    1957: Stratford East.
    1960: Aldwych.
  The White Devil
    1961: Old Vic (single performance).
'Beaumont and Fletcher'
  The Knight of the Burning Pestle
    1960: Royal Academy of Dramatic Art.
  The Maid's Tragedy
    1954: Bristol University Dramatic Society.
    1964: Mermaid.
  The Wild Goose Chase
    1958: Farnham Repertory.
  The Chances
    1962: Chichester.
  The Two Noble Kinsmen (? Fletcher and Shakespeare).
    1959: Reading University Dramatic Society.
  Cardenio (? Fletcher and Shakespeare)
    1955: Northampton Drama Club.
Thomas Heywood
  A Woman Killed with Kindness
    1961: Marlowe Society at Southwark.
John Ford
  'Tis Pity She's a Whore
    1956: Leeds University Union Theatre Group.
    1961: Mermaid.

The Broken Heart
   1959: Queen's University of Belfast Dramatic Society.
   1962: Chichester.
The Witch of Edmonton (with Dekker and Rowley)
   1962: Mermaid.
Philip Massinger
  The City Madam
   1964: Birmingham Repertory.
Sir William D'Avenant
  The Wits
   1963: Pitlochry Festival.
John Milton
  Comus
   1954: Birmingham School of Speech Training at Coventry.
   1958: Ludlow Festival.

1660–1700
John Dryden
  All for Love
   1955: Leatherhead Repertory.
   1958: Oxford University Dramatic Society.
   1960: Talisman Theatre Players, Kenilworth.
  The Tempest (with D'Avenant)
   1959: Old Vic.
John Milton
  Samson Agonistes
   1956: Phoenix Theatre Group at Birmingham Repertory.
   1965: Yvonne Arnaud, Guildford.
Thomas Otway
  The Soldier's Fortune
   1964: Playhouse, Oxford.
Sir George Etherege
  The Man of Mode
   1965: Georgian, Richmond.
William Wycherley
  The Gentleman Dancing Master
   1963: New, Oxford.
  The Country Wife
   1955: Stratford East.
   1956: Royal Court.
William Congreve
  The Double Dealer
   1959: Old Vic.
  Love for Love
   1965: National Theatre.
  The Way of the World
   1954: Theatre Royal, Windsor.
   1956: Saville.

George Villiers
   The Rehearsal
      1959 : Hovenden Theatre Club.

1700–1800
   Sir John Vanbrugh
      The Provok'd Wife
         1963 : Playhouse, Oxford, and Vaudeville.
      The Confederacy
         1964 : Playhouse, Oxford.
      The Relapse
         1954 : Richmond.
   George Farquhar
      The Recruiting Officer
         1956 : Bristol Old Vic.
         1961 : Unity.
         1963 : National Theatre.
      The Beaux' Stratagem
         1957 : Birmingham Repertory.
         1961 : Octagon Theatre Club, Bath (musical version).
         1963 : Ashcroft, Croydon.
   Susannah Centlivre
      A Bold Stroke for a Wife
         1954 : Questors.
      The Wonder
         1959 : Pitlochry Festival.
   Nicholas Rowe
      Jane Shore
         1962 : Hovenden Theatre Club.
   Colley Cibber
      She Would and She Would Not
         1955 : Salisbury Playhouse.
      The Comical Lovers
         1963 : Questors.
   John Gay
      The Beggar's Opera
         1963 : Aldwych.
   Joseph Addison
      The Drummer
         1961 : Hovenden Theatre Club.
   Joseph Reed
      The Register Office
         1956 : Hovenden Theatre Club.
   David Garrick
      Katharine and Petruchio
         1960 : Pitlochry Festival.

The Lying Valet
1957 : Hovenden Theatre Club.
The Clandestine Marriage (with George Colman the Elder)
1956 : Birmingham Repertory.
Henry Fielding
Tom Thumb
1960 : Cambridge University Mummers.
R. B. Sheridan
The Rivals
1956 : Lyceum, Edinburgh, later transferred to Saville.
Bristol Old Vic.
1961 : Pembroke, Croydon.
1963 : Lyric, Hammersmith.
The School for Scandal
1961 : Nonentities at Kidderminster.
1962 : Haymarket.
The Duenna
1954 : Wimbledon.
Oliver Goldsmith
The Good-Natur'd Man
1960 : Tavistock Repertory.
She Stoops to Conquer
1956 : Pitlochry Festival.
1960 : Old Vic.
1965 : Bristol Old Vic at Theatre Royal, Bath.
Arthur Murphy
All in the Wrong
1955 : Guildhall School of Music and Drama.
1956 : Toynbee Hall.
Thomas Holcroft
The Road to Ruin
1954 : Bristol Old Vic.
Isaac Bickerstaffe
The Sultan
1955 : Hovenden Theatre Club.
Lionel and Clarissa
1965 : Yvonne Arnaud, Guildford.

1800–1880
[Various revivals of melodramas, notably *Sweeny Todd* and *Maria Marten*, in adapted forms are here omitted, as are the frequent performances of the Savoy Operas.]
P. B. Shelley
The Cenci
1959 : Old Vic.
Dion Boucicault
The Colleen Bawn
1954 : Portcullis Theatre.

W. B. Rhodes
Bombastes Furioso
1957 : Theatre Royal, Margate.
W. S. Gilbert
Broken Hearts
1955 : Hovenden Theatre Club.
C. H. Hazlewood
Lady Audley's Secret
1964 : New Arts.
J. M. Morton
Cox and Box
1961 : Royal Court.
Tom Robertson
Caste
1955 : Connaught, Worthing.
Theatre Royal, Windsor (musical version).
Birmingham Repertory.
School
1957 : Birmingham Repertory (musical version).
1958 : same production at Prince's.
Tom Taylor
The Ticket-of-Leave Man
1956 : Arts.

1880–1900
[Plays written by Bernard Shaw and Sir James Barrie during this
period are included in the following (1900-30) section.]
Sir Charles Hawtrey
The Private Secretary
1954 : Arts.
1960 : Pitlochry Festival.
Brandon Thomas
Charley's Aunt
1954 : New.
H. A. Jones
The Silver King
1958 : Players'.
Sir Arthur Wing Pinero
The Magistrate
1959 : Old Vic.
1965 : Pitlochry Festival.
Dandy Dick
1955 : Pitlochry Festival.
1965 : Mermaid.
The Schoolmistress
1964 : Savoy.

The Amazons
  1954: Academy Theatre Group at New Lindsey.
The Second Mrs Tanqueray
  1961: Pembroke, Croydon.
Trelawny of the 'Wells'
  1965: National Theatre.
Oscar Wilde
  An Ideal Husband
    1959: Pitlochry Festival.
    1965: Opera House, Manchester, later presented at the Strand.
  The Importance of Being Earnest
    1959: Old Vic.
    1964: Arts, Cambridge.
    1965: Ashcroft, Croydon.
  Salomé
    1954: Q, transferred to St Martin's.
  A Florentine Tragedy
    1964: Little Theatre Club.

1900–1930
  Sir James Barrie
    Walker, London
      1962: Birmingham Repertory (musical version).
    The Admirable Crichton
      1960: Pitlochry Festival.
      1964: Shaftesbury (as *Our Man Crichton*, a musical version).
    The Boy David
      1954: Pitlochry Festival.
    What Every Woman Knows
      1960: Old Vic.
    Mary Rose
      1961: Pitlochry Festival.
      (Various Christmas productions of the popular *Peter Pan* are not listed here.)
  George Bernard Shaw
    Caesar and Cleopatra
      1956: Birmingham Repertory Theatre.
      1961: Duchess.
    Widowers' Houses
      1956: Merseyside Unity.
      1965: Stage Sixty at Stratford East.
    Mrs Warren's Profession
      1956: New London Theatre Group at the Royal Court.
      1965: Hampstead Theatre Club.
    Candida
      1960: Piccadilly.

Androcles and the Lion
 1960: Unity.
 1961: Mermaid.
The Devil's Disciple
 1956: Winter Garden.
 1965: Yvonne Arnaud, Guildford.
Arms and the Man
 1955: Pitlochry Festival.
 1962: Mermaid.
 1965: Playhouse, Chester.
The Shewing Up of Blanco Posnet
 1961: Mermaid.
The Doctor's Dilemma
 1956: Saville.
Captain Brassbound's Conversion
 1956: Stratford East.
 1958: Bristol Old Vic.
 1965: Meadow Players at Playhouse, Oxford.
You Never Can Tell
 1955: Birmingham Repertory.
Getting Married
 1965: Arts, Cambridge.
Fanny's First Play
 1956: Lyceum, Edinburgh.
 1965: Mermaid.
Major Barbara
 1956: Bristol Old Vic.
 1958: Royal Court.
Man and Superman
 1958: Bristol Old Vic.
 1965: New Arts.
Misalliance
 1956: Pitlochry Festival.
   Lyric, Hammersmith.
 1962: Meadow Players at Playhouse, Oxford.
 1963: Royal Court (Oxford production).
Pygmalion
 1957: Bristol Old Vic.
 1960: Pembroke, Croydon.
 1962: Pitlochry Festival.
Saint Joan
 1954: Arts (transferred to St Martin's, 1955).
 1955: Library Theatre, Manchester.
 1960: Old Vic.
 1963: National Theatre.
Heartbreak House
 1961: Playhouse, Oxford, later presented at Wyndham's.

M

The Apple Cart
1965 : Arts, Cambridge.
Too True to Be Good
1965 : Edinburgh Festival, and Strand.
J. E. Flecker
Hassan
1954 : Canterbury Festival.
John Galsworthy
Strife
1962 : Tavistock Repertory.
J. R. Ackerley
Prisoners of War
1955 : Irving.
R. C. Sherriff
Journey's End
1954 : New Torch.
Margaret Kennedy (with Basil Dean)
The Constant Nymph
1954 : Q.
Arnold Ridley
The Ghost Train
1958 : Pitlochry Festival.
W. Somerset Maugham
The Circle
1961 : Pitlochry Festival.
1965 : Ashcroft, Croydon, and Savoy.
St John Hankin
The Constant Lover
1962 : Hovenden Theatre Club.
Harold Brighouse
Hobson's Choice
1964 : National Theatre.
Ian Hay
The Housemaster
1954 : St Martin's.
      Pitlochry Festival.
Ben Travers
A Cuckoo in the Nest
1964 : Royal Court.
Rookery Nook
1964 : New, Oxford.
Thark
1965 : Yvonne Arnaud, Guildford, later presented at the Garrick.
Noël Coward
The Vortex
1965 : Yvonne Arnaud, Guildford.
Hay Fever
1964 : National Theatre.

Private Lives
    1954 : Regal Theatre, St Leonard's-on-Sea.
    1963 : Hampstead Theatre Club.
T. S. Eliot
  Murder in the Cathedral
    1954 : Bristol Old Vic.
    1961 : Lambeth Dramatic Club at Edinburgh.
    1965 : Pitlochry Festival.
James Bridie
  The Anatomist
    1956 : Gateway, Edinburgh.
  The Switchback
    1959 : Pitlochry Festival.
  Tobias and the Angel
    1960 : Bankside Players at Regent's Park.
  The King of Nowhere
    1965 : Pitlochry Festival.

Index